The Complete Guide to Surfing

Also by Peter Dixon

Men Who Ride Mountains

The Complete Guide to Surfing

Peter Dixon

The Lyons Press
Guilford, Connecticut
An imprint of The Globe Pequot Press

The Lyons Press is an imprint of The Globe Pequot Press.

Printed in the United States of America

10 9 8 7 6 5 4 3 2 1

Design by Compset, Inc.

The Library of Congress Cataloging-in-Publication Data

Dixon, Peter L.
    The complete guide to surfing / Peter Dixon.
        p. cm.
    Includes bibliographical references (p. 191) and index.
    ISBN 1-58574-346-1
    1. Surfing.   I. Title.

GV840.S8 D515 2001
797.3'2—dc21
                                                    2001050198

To Sarah, who surfs through life with me.

Contents

Foreword

Despite having been a surfer myself for close to forty years, and despite how many surfers there are now worldwide—an estimated 15 million or more—I have known very few real surfers. By that I mean surfers whose lives have been lived in accordance to the natural rhythms and beauty of the ocean. Peter Dixon is one such real surfer.

Born in New York City (it wasn't his fault), he soon found his way to Southern California, and then to the Malibu area, where he began lifeguarding, diving, and surfing in the late 1940s. More than 50 years later, he's still at it, perfecting the aquatic arts, surfing, and living an ocean-centered life. He lives in a suitably unconventional, eight-sided beachside house in Malibu, just a short walk from one of the last remaining truly secret surf spots in Southern California. He positively chirps at the thought of the next wave he will catch there. He met his wife, Sarah, in the surf (they literally ran into each other while body-surfing), and they raised a family of three children, all of whom grew up to be surfers.

Truth be told, all successful surfers—those who have found a way to continue to enjoy surfing throughout their lives—are scam artists. How else to escape the yoke of the land-based, workaday world? Peter has mastered the art of finding ways to make a living that add to, not detract from, his aquatic pleasures. For a surfer, going to school and getting a great education, Peter would agree, is indispensable. But why slave away in school on something you care little about when you can do as Peter did when he finagled UCLA to let him do his master's thesis on developing safety criteria for skin and scuba divers? Translation: water time for Peter.

His career as a television and screenwriter is equally illustrative. Let's measure the water time: writing the first episode of *Flipper* (plus twelve more), episodes for *Sea Hunt*, creating and writing *Sea Lab 2020* and more recently *Danger Bay* (a series for Disney that ran for six years in over sixty countries), and, finally, some years back, the sheer brilliance of selling Universal a pilot entitled *Raymond Burr in Fiji*. God, you have to love Peter. He also edited and wrote for various surfing magazines, but those are such pedestrian, obvious means for a surfer.

His greatest coup is the book you're holding. *The Complete Guide to Surfing* is the culmination of more than 35 years of polishing, refining, updating, and expanding what was the best-selling surfing book in history, with more than 350,000 copies in print. It is the distillation, the essence, of thirty-five more years of Peter's life on and in the water. His *Complete Book of Surfing*, published in 1965, was *the* book to get. (You can still find tattered copies on the shelves of Midwestern libraries, where it has been the training manual for generations of hodads.) I still have the copy my parents gave me that year as a Christmas present (shopping for a young surfer is easy if you accept rather than discourage his pursuit). At the time I was more of a bodysurfer than a standup surfer, and Peter's book was the first time I'd seen all forms of surfing treated equally—such is his egalitarian nature.

In 1986 I organized the first-ever conference on the medical aspects of surfing, which then led to the founding of the Surfer's Medical Association—still a thriving international association. The two-week conference was held in Tavarua, Fiji (surf by day, seminars by night—right from the Peter Dixon playbook). I invited expert speakers, all surfing health professionals, to cover the pathogenic aspects of surfing, such as injuries (back, shoulder, and knee soft-tissue injuries are common among surfers, though fractures, spinal cord injuries, and deaths are not), surfer's ear (bony growths in the outer ear canal, an epidemic among surfers), and such topics as surfing dermatology and ophthalmology. But I also wanted an authority on healthy surfing, someone who could teach us about the salubrious side of surfing. That person was Peter. Although he was not a physician, it was clear that he knew more than anyone else on the subject: This book, and really all his books, are treatises on healthy surfing.

The updating and expansion—the redux—of his 1965 book has been a continual process for Peter. Each day he surfs, he learns or notices something new about the ocean. While numerous other books on surfing by other authors have since been published, none represents Peter's experience or authenticity.

This book begins with the phrase: "The surfer's wet-and-wild world," which will either make you cheer or cringe. Cringe if you've been co-opted and jaded by the advertising industry that has been using the surfing lifestyle—and its best phrases—to sell garbage for years; cheer if you realize that Peter is the one who originated these expressions, and that, verily, this entire book is stuffed full of such sweetness.

—Mark "Doc Hazard" Renneker, M.D.
Associate Clinical Professor
University of California, San Francisco

Acknowledgments

Without the ocean, the winds, and the Earth's shores, there would be no surfing. So first of all I thank nature for making our sport possible. We who surf must also honor those long-ago pioneers, who in some distant sea paddled down a wave, stood, and found glory in the surf. Today, I thank all the wave-riders I've surfed with and especially those who said, "Your wave, Pete."

To bring this book to life, I'm forever indebted to Bernie Baker for his photographic art. Despite his busy schedule, Bernie always had time to take one more image or look deeper in his photo files. My family—Sarah, Pahl, Jamie, and Megan—all gave their time and skill to hone the manuscript and guide me through creating my first book in cyberspace. Tony Lyons, who published this book, caught my vision from the very first. Tom McCarthy, my insightful and inspiring editor, gave invaluable suggestions and kept me on track. Everyone I asked for help—be it advice, photos, personal recollections, introductions—all responded with immediate enthusiasm. I'm blessed to have known you all.

Peter Dixon
Malibu, California, 2001

Introduction

The surfer's wet-and-wild world has changed greatly since I first began riding waves. Back then, fiberglass-covered balsawood surfboards were being phased out in favor of foam-core boards. Moviegoers were packing theaters to see *Gidget* and *The Endless Summer*, and Malibu's Surfrider Beach was becoming the Mecca for every wannabe wave-rider. Highly skilled big-wave surfers were just beginning their migration to Oahu's North Shore to challenge the heavies at Makaha, Waimea, the Pipeline, and Sunset Beach.

It was a time of transition and ferment: transition as surfing's popularity was about to explode and go commercial; ferment because the old-timers and the newcomers were in conflict over surf territory—a natural course of events exhibited in many suddenly popular, mass-appeal action sports, such as skiing, in-line skating, skateboarding, and sailboarding.

When Malibu became "The Malibu" in the early 1960s, the greater Southern California population was about three and a half million people. Today, some 20 million people live within easy driving distance of Malibu and most surfing beaches. The waves have become crowded, gridlocked. All those people, all those toilets being flushed, all those factories, cars, and households discharging pollutants, tend to poison the air and waters near urban centers like Los Angeles. Unclean water leads to illness, crowded waves create stress, and commercialism sullies the sport's purity. Surfers need to be leaders in the fight to respect the ocean and keep the water we play in healthy.

Let's go back to when I first began writing about surfing. Here's how it began for me, sitting in a damp storage room with my fingers on the keys of a rusting Olivetti typewriter. Just outside my "office," 10 yards from the ocean at Topanga Beach, California, the surf crashed on the shore, shaking my desk. It was time to write about something I loved deeply, and I began, "The sport of surfing originated . . ."

Decades later, in a new century, the swells still roll in from the distant horizon. A million surfers stare seaward, anticipating that magic moment when we're one with the wave, riding tall and proud for shore.

Nothing has changed, yet everything has changed. Like yesterday, young surfers struggle to earn a place in the lineup, and the 100 or so truly accomplished big-wave riders are challenging 50-foot giants. Despite the passage of time, surfing is still about having fun.

There is simply no way to express the feeling a good ride on a big, fast-moving wave brings to surfers. Some surfers get stoked, others are exhilarated, a few are blasted, but most feel deeply satisfied that the wave was perfect and the ride long. New surfers are beginning a sport that started many hundreds of years ago in Polynesia, and after a period of dormancy, reborn. Surfing's appeal is now global, with surfers challenging the waves from Australia to Atlantic City, from Hawaii to Peru, and from South Africa to Malibu.

Why the enduring interest? What draws people into the cold water, to the pounding waves, to the hazards of cuts on sharp coral and collisions with other surfers? Why do surfers fly and drive and sail thousands of miles to be blasted off their boards by a wave? Why have millions worldwide bought or built boards? And finally, what is there about surfing that captures the imagination and satisfies some basic need of mind and body?

There are several qualities of surfing that might provide some answers. Surfing is the most individualistic of all sports. Alone on a board, charging across a wave at 15 or 20 miles an hour, the surfer experiences an ecstatic communication with natural forces, a delicious isolation, and total freedom from the anxieties and mundanities of the workaday world.

Surfing is a challenge requiring intense concentration. The surfer's senses are totally engaged in keeping one's body in balance and the wave from dominating the ride. This is particularly true in big surf. On smaller, well-formed waves, there may be time to look around, wave to a friend, and plan ahead. But the surfer who lets his attention lag will lose the wave. Waves are living, moving things, and like people, no two are alike. This infinite variety gives surfing color, excitement, action. Yet surfing is uncomplicated. In the frightfully complex world of modern technology, nothing is quite as refreshingly simple as a functional surfboard and waves, sun, and sky.

Surfers as a rule are not the anxious sort. I've never worried sitting on a surfboard waiting for a wave, and I've rarely known a surfer who was troubled out on the water. This escape from the ordinary is certainly part of surfing, as is the feeling of being unique. Many old-timers have observed that younger surfers start the sport because of the status it brings them. But whatever the motivation, the surfer still faces the sea and waves.

Some of the famous Hawaiian-based big-wave riders feel compelled to challenge the surf; they see this flirtation with accident and death as a striving for power over nature. One famous big-waver claims that riding mountain-size waves gives him a feeling of immortality.

Others are attracted by the grinding cameras of surf filmmakers and the admiring throng on the beach.

Surfing's popularity has created problems. The high demand for surfing areas has resulted in crowded waves at most accessible beaches, and the dangers of collision and hard wipeouts are ever present. Learning to surf well adds to the safety and enjoyment of the sport. The beginner needs to practice, and practice hard if he or she wants to become expert. There are no shortcuts around actual experience on a board, but some of the knowledge gained by others can be passed on to the new surfer. I've written this book to help smooth the way and provide a better understanding of what happens when surfer and wave meet.

Large numbers of surfers means bigness, and bigness means that surfing becomes less free and more organized. The speed and frequency of jet travel permits surfers easy access to almost all the big-wave beaches of the world. Surfers leave more than footprints behind. They leave their cultural impact, their money, and a desire among the young locals to become surfers themselves.

The continued growth of surfing has also resulted in specialization. There is a growing division between professional and amateur surfers, between short and longboarders, big-wave riders and hot-doggers. Professional surfers, sponsored by business groups, are the heroes of the sport, and many earn a very comfortable living riding waves on the international circuit.

The sight of surfers sliding waves is commonplace along the shores of wherever waves break. Australian, South American, South African, French, Mexican, Japanese, Brazilian, Indian, Israeli, and English surfers are all riding waves in international competition. Despite this attention to the highly profiled, though, the recreational surfer predominates. Surfboard shops continue to pour out millions of gleaming boards, and a growing industry has emerged to cater to surfers' needs. Before long, surfing will become an Olympic sport.

Surfing's evolution has been both positive and negative. Surfers have become powerful, visual symbols of individualism, of freedom from conformity. Sadly, a few surfers have digressed into tribal, Neanderthal punks who defend their local surf turf with violence. Localism is the harmful opposite of surfing's Aloha Spirit of sharing. Why surf if that wonderful flowing energy that comes from riding a nature-made wave is spoiled by the bad vibrations of localism?

We who surf put so much of ourselves into gaining those exquisite moments of peak experience. There's no other sport that requires so little gear yet gives so much in terms of excitement, challenge, and soul satisfaction. After a surfing session, all you've left behind are footprints in the sand that the tide will soon wash away. What you've taken away is a very special gift that needs to be respected and protected. With that, let's go surfing.

The Complete Guide to Surfing

Surfing's Rich Legacy

The first people to capture the energy of a breaking wave and use if for pleasure were likely Polynesians living in Tahiti and Bora Bora, in the vast emptiness of sea and islands in the western Pacific Ocean we now call Oceania. Sometime between A.D. 800 and 1100, an adventurous group of these Polynesians, fleeing increasingly crowded conditions on their isolated islands, sailed off in search of a better life. Navigating by clues from sun, moon, stars, currents, and the flight of sea birds, they sailed northeastward, seeking new lands to settle. Their epic migration across the central Pacific took these highly skilled seafarers to the Hawaiian Islands, a journey of perhaps five thousand miles. At the mercy of winds and currents the voyage required enormous skill, courage, and tenacity to reach a landfall.

Stowed in the hulls of their giant sailing catamarans were the prototypes of today's modern surfboard. Though none has survived the ravages of time, these

First drawing of a surfer, from Wm. Ellis, Polynesian Researches, 1831. Dixon Collection

primitive boards most likely were short, about six feet or so, enough to support a highly skilled stand-up surfer. Surfing as we know it was invented and refined in Hawaii, but the sport's antecedents began in Oceania with the Polynesians. When HMS *Bounty* dropped anchor off Tahiti in 1779, English sailors witnessed men, women, and children

Early Hawaiian surfboards displayed at the Bishop Museum, Honolulu. The longest is a 16-foot olo, surfed by royalty. One of Duke Kahanamoku's wooden boards, of the shorter akaia design, stands on the right. Bishop Museum Photo

riding waves on short wooden planks. The ship's boatswain's mate, James Morrison, observed how little Tahitian children "also take their sport in the smaller surfs."

The Polynesians found the Hawaiian Islands a bountiful land, and their culture flourished. The new Hawaiians discovered an abundance of the spilling surf needed to ride their boards off many points and beaches, and as their surfing skills improved their boards grew longer and more sophisticated. Over the years these early Polynesians perfected wave-riding and accorded ritual and meaning to the sport that enriched the lives of both royalty and commoners.

Surfing in pre-European Hawaii was an important part of everyday life and culture, with strong class overtones. Longer, better-riding boards and the best surfing breaks were reserved for members of the ruling class, the *alii*. These long boards, called *olos*, could reach 16 feet and weigh as much as 150 pounds. Commoners used shorter boards, called *akaias*, which were about eight feet long. Children surfed little planks called *paipos*, similar to today's bodyboards. A commoner found using an *olo* or surfing a royal break could be put to death. Various royal families engaged in surfing competitions, often with high-stakes betting on the outcome. Some chiefs would wager several double-hulled sailing canoes.

Building a surfboard required that certain rituals be performed when the lightweight koa tree was cut, when the wood shaped, and before the new surfboard was launched. When the surf was up, work stopped, and everyone paddled out. Both royalty and commoners treated their boards with care and respect. After surfing, the boards were dried, rubbed down with kukui nut oil and carefully stored out of the sun.

Western Eyes

In 1778, a British lookout atop the mast of Captain James Cook's ship *Resolution* first set eyes on Hawaii. As the great English seaman and explorer sailed into Kealakekua Bay on the island of Hawaii, his astonished crew sighted some men who appeared to be flying over the water. What they saw were Hawaiian nobility, surfing on their longboard *olos*. To an Englishman of the eighteenth century, the tall, impressive Hawaiians standing erect and riding huge waves across the blue water of a tropical bay must have been a wondrous sight.

A most impressed Lieutenant James King, a member of Cook's crew, writes of his impressions of surfing in Captain Cook's *A Voyage to the Pacific Ocean*, Volume III:

> Whenever, from stormy weather, or any extraordinary swell at sea, the impetuosity of the surf is increased to its utmost height, they

choose that time for this amusement which is performed in the following manner: twenty or thirty of the natives, taking each a long narrow board, rounded at the ends, set out together from shore. The first wave they meet, they plunge under, and suffering to roll over them, rise again beyond it, and make the rest of their way by swimming, out to sea. The second wave is encountered in the same manner with the first; the great difficulty consisting of seizing the proper moment of diving under it, which, if missed, the person is caught by the surf, and driven back again with great violence; and all his dexterity is then required to prevent himself from being dashed against the rocks. As soon as they have gained, by these repeated efforts, the smooth water beyond the surf, they lay themselves at length on their board, and prepare for their return. As the surf consists of a number of waves, of which every third is remarked to be always larger than the other, and to flow higher on the shore, the rest breaking in the immediate space, their first object is to place themselves on the summit of the largest surge, by which they are driven along with amazing rapidity toward the shore.

Lieutenant King concludes by writing, "The boldness and address, with which they perform these difficult and dangerous maneuvers, was altogether astonishing, and is scarce to be credited." King's report also describes female surfers and canoe paddlers catching waves.

Hawaiians continued surfing mostly without distraction from outsiders until the 1820s, when new invaders began to erode their rich traditions. Yankee and European whalers brought with them disruptions and disease, and much of Hawaiian culture was irrevocably damaged by growing Western influence. In the years following Cook's first visit, the island population was devastated by diseases for which they had no natural immunity. Smallpox, measles, and sexually transmitted infections would kill huge numbers of islanders. One hundred years after Cook's landfall, Hawaii's population had dropped from some 400,000 people to about 40,000—an astounding ninety percent reduction.

The islands' rich surfing traditions faced a further assault beginning in 1821, when the islanders received a well-meaning gift from the "civilized" world—Calvinist missionaries from Boston bringing their restrictive brand of Christianity.

The impact of disease, missionary zeal, and economic exploitation upon Hawaiian culture almost brought an end to surfing in the islands. Missionaries called for muumuus and trousers to cover the natives' bodies, introduced guilt and sin to cloud their souls, then banned the hula and the music and sport that kept the Hawaiians healthy and happy. Briefly, in 1888, under the rule of King Kalakaua, surfing enjoyed a revival. But in short time the sport was again suppressed by the impact of commerce, as lucrative and growing industries such as sugar plantations and land development, and the accompanying political power that grew with them, further eroded traditional Hawaiian culture. The annexation of Hawaii by the United States in 1898 solidified Western influence.

A Turn-of-the-Century Revival

Still, the lure of the waves off Waikiki continued to draw the daring and adventurous. As the new century dawned, the rolling, easily caught surf off Waikiki did more to insure surfing's survival than anything else. As Honolulu grew rapidly, people were drawn to the beach at Waikiki, where the last of the Hawaiian surfers still practiced their ancient sport. Local *haoles* (non-Hawaiians) were inspired to try surfing by the long, graceful rides of the Hawaiian wave riders.

The first surf clubs were started in the early decades of the twentieth century, when hotels, tourism, and commerce were developing in and around Waikiki. The Hawaiian Outrigger Canoe Club was founded in 1908 to preserve and promote "surfing on boards and in Hawaiian outrigger canoes." Its members were mostly haoles. Three years later the Hui Nalu Surf Club was formed with mostly Hawaiian members. By the time the enormously popular writer Jack London surfed his first Waikiki wave in 1915, the Outrigger Canoe Club had 1,200 members.

The turn of the century also saw a relaxation of missionary influence, and young people could show their bodies again, although swimsuits still covered most of one's skin. This new era brought with it a revival of the ancient sport. Perhaps the greatest proponent of the surfing resurgence was one of the most famous modern Hawaiians, Duke Kahanamoku, the world's fastest swimmer. As a freestyle sprint swimmer, the Duke competed in the 1912, 1920, 1924, and 1928 Olympics, bringing back a gold medal and several silver medals to Hawaii. A superb athlete, he almost qualified for the 1932 Olympics in Los Angeles, which he attended as a non-playing captain of the Hawaiian water polo team.

His Olympic success brought the Duke worldwide celebrity, and his surfing sparked attention and enthusiasm for the sport on both coasts of the American mainland and in Australia and New Zealand, where he became the first to demonstrate that one could ride across the face of a wave as well as straight ahead.

The pride in swimming and surfing that the Duke brought back to the islands from his international travels, and the work he and his four brothers did to form surfing clubs, helped greatly to ensure that the sport would not die again. I met Duke three times while editor of the long-gone *Surfing Illustrated* magazine. He was always gracious, friendly, and willing to give his time to support surfing and encourage young people to take up the sport that meant so much to him and his people.

The Duke, then the world's fastest swimmer, brought an Olympic gold medal back to Hawaii in 1912, and surfing to much of the world. Bishop Museum Photo

If you'd like to get the flavor and feel of surfing just after the turn of the twentieth century, read Jack London's "A Royal Sport: Surfing at Waikiki," published in 1907 in *A Woman's Home Companion* and later included as a chapter in his *Cruise of the Snark*. In the heavy prose style of the time, London describes how he learned to surf and what it was like living on Waikiki Beach. As London learned to surf Hawaiian

The Duke about to award trophies to the finalists of the first Duke Kahanamoku Surfing Championships, 1967. Beside The Duke are Fred Van Dyke and Butch Van Arts-dalen. Diamond Head rises in the background. Dixon Photo

style, he met and wrote about another man who helped bring surfing to the mainland:

> Out there in the midst . . . of the big smoky ones, a third man was added to our part, one Freeth. Shaking water from my eyes as I emerged from one wave and peered ahead to see what the next one looked like, I saw him tearing in on the back of it, standing upright on his board, carelessly poised, a young bronzed god with a sunburn.

In California, the Pacific Electric (P&E) Railroad played an important role in bringing surfing to the mainland. Shortly before World War I, P&E began laying tracks throughout Southern California. These were the days of great suburban land booms, when developers were making fortunes (as they still do). In 1909, to entice the public to relocate where new lots were being offered for sale, the railroad hired George Freeth, an Irish-Hawaiian who was an extraordinarily talented swimmer and surfer, to put on a surfing exhibition at Redondo Beach. His wave-riding demonstrations up and down the California coast drew thousands of spectators, and gave surfing its start on the West Coast.

On his way to the 1912 Olympics, the Duke joined Freeth in California and gave surfing exhibitions from San Diego to Santa Barbara. His 500-yard ride at Corona del Mar thrilled the locals and inspired many to attempt surfing. The Duke then went to the East Coast, body-surfed the New York beaches, rode a board at New Jersey's Atlantic City pier, and became the first person to surf the Atlantic's waves. The Duke was the first and best ambassador surfing ever had. He truly represented the Hawaiian Aloha Spirit of respect for nature, humanity, and the sea.

The Beachboys

At Waikiki in the 1920s, an increasing number of young Hawaiians were again sliding rolling combers, which greatly impressed the growing invasion of tourists arriving by ship. Tourists spent money, and Hawaii's tourist-based economy began to boom. The profits from land and hotel development quickly transformed comfortable, uncongested Waikiki area into dense rows of tourist-serving hotels and businesses. The Hawaiians lost much of their original land to developers and were forced to work for the very people who took away their culture.

But tourists helped continue surfing's revival. The more adventurous visitors who had arrived on such ships as the Matson liner *Lurline* watched from the balconies of the pink Royal Hawaiian Hotel as locals rode the spilling waves and wanted to learn to surf. The Hawaiians,

Waikiki beachboys riding solid wooden boards, 1932. Their love of surfing helped keep the sport alive. Bishop Museum Photo

being hospitable and in need of employment, were quite happy to oblige. The 1920s saw the birth of the beachboy era, a tradition that continues today despite many other changes. Beachboys were more than surf coaches for sunburned tourists. They were Waikiki's first lifeguards, great canoe paddlers, carefree companions to all, and expert *watermen*, a term of respect often applied to surfers who are skilled swimmers, skin- and scuba-divers, paddlers, boatmen, and lifeguards. Watermen have a great knowledge of and a "feel" for the sea.

By the late 1940s, Waikiki, with its 12 major surf breaks, became the core element in surfing's explosive growth. Waikiki, by then ringed with tourist hotels, was the surf paradise of the Pacific. Nowhere else was it easier to learn to surf. Beachboys were always there to rent boards and paddle out with first-timers for an emotional lift and the thrill of standing up and riding a wave. Many of these watermen pioneered the way out to Makaha and Oahu's North Shore and were among the first to ride truly giant waves. When you surf Waikiki, and every surfer must make that pilgrimage, you'll be paying homage to the men who are a living link to surfing's past. My wife and I surfed Waikiki recently and found that the Aloha Spirit is still alive and well.

Makaha, 1949. Hawaiian North Shore surf pioneers with their hot curl big wave boards. Left to right: Russ Takahi, Rabbit KaKai, Wally Froiseth, and Roy Folk seated in Froiseth's classic 1936 Ford V8 Phaeton. Courtesy: Wally Froiseth

Many of the visitors who first learned to surf from beachboys became hooked and stayed in the islands. One of them was the great waterman Pete Peterson, surfing's "Iron Man."

Peterson, an early Santa Monica, California, beach lifeguard, first surfed Waikiki in the summer of 1932. When winter came and the surf off Waikiki didn't offer enough challenge, he and fellow lifeguard Lorren Harrison brought their 12-foot finless boards along on a hitchhiking exploration of Oahu's North Shore—before Oahu's country roads were paved. With the eyes of surfers, Peterson and Harrison saw the now-famous surfing breaks of Sunset Beach, Waimea, and the Pipeline for the first time. Awestruck, the pair knew they couldn't handle the surf they were watching. To get the feel of these powerful giants they swam out among the pounding waves, swimming nude just for the hell of it off beaches that had yet to see a single shack or building. They returned to Honolulu promising to come back with the right boards for those heavy, fast-moving waves. And they did some years later. But World War II interrupted their plans, and the North Shore wouldn't be ridden until the fighting ended. Peterson went on to become a pioneer skin- and scuba-diver and one of the first underwater film stuntmen.

Late 1950s, the day Waimea Bay was first surfed. Mike Stang is being blown off the wave top as Pat Curren bails out. Photo: Dr. Don James from Peter Dixon Collection.

He also won dozens of surfing and paddling contests in his long career as a waterman.

Evolving Surfboard Design

Surfboard design has continued to evolve and adapt to conditions since the times of the Polynesian voyagers. Surfing's modern era, and the new technologies and different ways of thinking that accompanied it, have brought with it a stream of new board configurations and designs.

Hauling a heavy board around is tiring, and early on surfers began what has been a continuous search for lighter, more maneuverable boards. In the late 1920s, Hawaiian waterman Tom Blake designed and built hollow, lightweight surfboards that were quite fast and paddled

Tom Blake, one of surfing's greats, stands by his quiver of solid and hollow boards. The influence of early Hawaii surfboard designs is readily apparent. Bishop Museum Photo

easily. Because Blake's finless boards were quite long, they didn't turn well. But this lack of maneuverability didn't prevent him from winning most of the surfing and paddling competitions he entered, since most of these events were held in easily surfed Waikiki waves, where radical turns were not necessary. His early boards were varnished hundred-pounders, but his later refinements brought the weight down to about 60 pounds. Blake's hollow-board design was later improved by a method that called for laminating strips of hard but lightweight redwood to even lighter balsa, which further reduced bulk and weight. The harder redwood was used along the board's edges, nose, and tail. In pre-fiberglass days, all boards were varnished to make them waterproof.

These composite boards were the most popular type in the years before World War II. (Many of these 10-foot redwood-balsa boards were later reshaped and shortened by the kids learning to surf after the war.)

Pete Peterson created a variation on the laminated balsa-redwood board when he returned to California from Hawaii in the mid-1930s and built a pair of very light all-balsa boards coated with several layers of varnish. Though the varnish cracked easily and provided little protection, the all-balsa surfboard idea was basically sound and an improvement on Blake's design because it was shorter, lighter and, with the addition of a fin, could be turned more easily.

The modern surfboard was born in the mid-1940s with the invention of fiberglass cloth and plastic resins, which boardbuilders laminated onto balsa blanks. By 1952 fiberglass-covered balsa boards were being produced commercially in Southern California by surf pioneers Joe Quigg, Mat Kivlin, Dale Velzy, and Bob Simmons. Simmons, an engineer, also developed a foam-filled board in 1946 from which today's types evolved.

Balsa had certain disadvantages, though some purists insist it has a different "feel" that produces a board that is easier to ride. The wood quickly became waterlogged if the fiberglass skin was fractured, and finding light, high-quality balsa was always a problem for surfboard builders. Shaping balsa blanks required the skill of a master woodworker and the eye of an artist. Unlike foam blanks, each glued up plank of balsa responded to the draw knife and power plane differently.

I once owned a remarkable 10-foot Simmons twin-fin board that had a foam core sandwiched between two layers of marine plywood covered with fiberglass. Another of his designs, this one short-lived, was a hollow all-fiberglass board that was so buoyant it became airborne on a wave and couldn't be controlled.

But in the pre-foam days, fiberglass-covered balsa boards represented a vast improvement over the redwood-balsa laminate design. A 10-foot balsa-fiberglass board weighed half as much as an identically sized redwood-balsa model and could be carried by the average man or woman. They paddled and turned easily, were much more buoyant for their size, and eminently more maneuverable. Surfers could now catch waves closer to the waves' curling shoulders, turn back into the break, and pull out before it collapsed around them. With balsa-fiberglass boards, surfers had a wave tool that allowed them to shift balance quickly and perform stylish maneuvers like hanging ten toes over the nose, riding in the curl of the wave, and carving sharp turns.

These shorter, lighter boards came of age at Surfrider Beach, Malibu, California, in the early 1950s, where most of these innovative maneuvers were first developed. In Australia, the term "Malibu board" is still used to describe any eight- to ten-foot style of fairly wide, round-nosed surfboard.

The lighter balsa boards helped many women become surfers. Hauling heavy pre-balsa boards down steep trails to the beach prevented all but the strongest women from surfing. Balsa—and later fiberglass—boards allowed women surfers to take their rightful place in the waves. Gender barriers have fallen and at most surf breaks, women are welcomed for the spirit and grace they give the sport. As Jericho Poppler Bartlow, one of the first professional women surfers and a dancer, recalled, "I think of surfing and waves as spontaneous, like dance, like music . . . if you can share it, that's even better."

Like Bartlow, most of the pioneer women surfers started riding waves on Malibu-type balsa boards. In the late 1950s, the surfers Marge Calhoun and Joyce Hoffman could handle Malibu overhead waves as well as anyone. Later Margo Oberg and Joyce Rell Sun would ride the Hawaiian heavies along with the men, but there was a difference. The women's style, skill, and grace seemed to put them in a pleasing balance with the waves. Women surfers tend to go with the flow rather that battling the break. Marilyn Edwards, surfer and publisher of *Wahine* magazine, noted that women surf with such fluid grace because there is a unique symbiotic relationship between them and water.

Surfing was changed forever with the advent of polyurethane foam, an ideal material for making surfboard blanks. The fiberglass-covered foam board was almost a magical discovery and launched surfing into its modern era. The first foam boards were designed and manufactured by Hobie Alter and his friend "Grubby" Clark back in 1958. Within a year, foam boards had revolutionized the surfboard industry and demand skyrocketed. Foam blanks were vastly easier to shape. The consistency of foam and the ease with which it could be power-planed and sanded speeded production and lowered manufacturing costs. Some early boardbuilders developed semiautomated machines to carve out the basic dimensions before hand-finishing. As hoards of young people took to the waves, an increasing number of surf shops opened along both coasts of the United States.

The Australian Connection

The catalyst and igniter of the Australian "new wave" era of short surfboard design was George Greenough, a quiet young Californian from Santa Barbara who had enough money to make several trips Down Under and to finance building his many surfboard design concepts. The Australians and Greenough hit it off quickly and found mutual respect. Greenough was, and still is, a surfing wizard and the most adept kneeboard surfer in the world. On his many visits to Australia, Greenough shared his advanced thinking on short surfboards and flexible fin design with Bob McTavish and several others who took the art of surfboard building seriously. As Greenough offered suggestions, McTavish would incorporate them in experimental surfboards. Luckily, McTavish had the talent of a master shaper and could translate Greenough's concepts to foam and fiberglass. At first it was hard to paddle out from the American surfing influence, but George was after something better. He would tell his down-under friends, "Forget the crap in the American surf magazines, do it your own way."

These brainstorming surfing sessions and cooperative designs worked. Soon McTavish and Greenough were ripping on their revolutionary shortboards and coaching other board makers by having them

Nat Young in the 1960s, then Australian and World Surfing Champion, cranks a radical turn riding a Bob McTavish/George Greenough design short board at Long Reef, Australia. Photo: Alby Falzon from Dixon Collection

alter the shape a little here, a little there. As the boards grew shorter and wider, McTavish the test pilot would paddle out to prove (or not) that Greenough's vision worked. From these sessions came the hooked fin, V-bottoms, and kick-nosed surfboards.

Today, ongoing global research and development of the modern shortboard has crossed over to longboarding, with the same board design features and high-amplitude maneuvers being expressed in a larger format. Hotdoggers of all ages are cranking huge turns and blasting off the lip on nine-foot-plus boards as well as noseriding or just trimming with classic style.

The Malibu Scene

Malibu's Surfrider Beach was the birthplace of Southern California surfing culture. The Malibu scene between 1950 and 1960 was a special place of sand and surf. That colorful 350-yard stretch of curving beach and its mix of eccentric characters had a unique flavor found nowhere else in the surfing world. Besides the wonderfully shaped and consistent waves, there was the glamour of this seaside community that is home to movie and television elite.

Malibu also meant freedom for most who gathered there—freedom in the surf and freedom from the constraints of conventional, uptight 1950s society. It was an "in" place without obvious status symbols. How well you surfed was what really counted. But most of all, Malibu was good surf and fun times at a very special beach where the crowd was mellow and hooted approval for a wave well ridden. Hanging out at Malibu meant meeting friends, girls in bikinis, cracking open a beer or a watermelon and later washing off the juice in the waves. Surfing as a cultural phenomenon came of age here and the fun and good times continue today, despite the crowds.

By 1960, many of the big-wave pioneers who began surfing at Malibu became fed up with the crowds and made the ultracheap ($76 one way) U.S. Overseas Airways DC-6 propeller plane flight to Hawaii for the big surf. On their balsa boards, early lifeguard-surfers Peter Cole, Ricky Grigg, Buzzy Trent, and Mike Stange learned the basics of big-wave surfing. Later these four, along with local Hawaiians George Downing, Jose Angel, Kimo Hollinger, and others would be the first to ride the thundering surf off Makaha, Sunset Beach, Waimea Bay, and other North Shore giant wave breaks.

Malibu was where Gidget and Tubesteak hung out at the famous shack, where Mickey Dora and Johnny Fain dueled in the surf, and hundreds of surf products, and even an automobile, found a name. Gidget was 15-year-old Kathy Kohner, who kept a diary about the wild

Malibu, a summer day, early 1960s when longboards ruled the waves. Dixon photo

goings-on at Malibu and how she wrangled her way into the band of early 1950s Malibu surfers to become part of the fun-loving crew. Her father, writer Frederick Kohner, used her diary as the background for his successful 1957 novel *Gidget,* and another Malibu legend was born. Tubesteak, whose given name was Terry Tracey, was so named because of his ability to down an enormous amount of hot dogs. He was the unofficial leader of the surf crew who lived in the beach shack.

Dora and Fain also became surfing legends. Each had an individual style that stood out in the waves. Dora was smooth and poised, almost ballet-dancer graceful on a wave. Fain ripped the surf with his aggressive turns and nobody liked to get in his way. Dora was well spoken, a mysterious gentleman for another age. Fain, a blustering street kid, would challenge anyone for a wave and most would back off, except for Dora. For five years they fought for top spot in the Malibu surfers' hierarchy. As the crowds of wannabe surfers jammed the waves, the Dora and Fain duels ended. Fain remained at Malibu. The enigmatic Dora traveled the world, and his legend has yet to end.

The mystique of Malibu—with help from surfing films like Grant Rholof's 1964 award-winning short, *Wet and Wild,* and Bruce Brown's classic 1966 *Endless Summer*—created the surfing boom that began in the late 1950s and has yet to peak. (For a detailed account of Malibu's surfing history, see the author's *Men Who Ride Mountains,* published by The Lyons Press.)

The Malibu board, surf movies, and surf music all combined to jumpstart what grew to become surfing's wide popularity. Old-time Malibu surfers saw the end of their era coming and many moved to the Hawaiian Islands or remote overseas beaches where the waves were less crowded.

A Worldwide Appeal

As the surfing population grew, and urban surfing breaks became increasingly crowded, wave-hungry young people began traveling to distant shores. Wave hunters found good surf off Biarritz, France, in South Africa, along the length of Peru, off Brazil, along the coast of most of Central America, off Japan, Indonesia, Tahiti, Fiji, and ringing almost all the tropical islands of the world. And, stay-at-home surfers saw it all in the growing numbers of surf films. Today there are few breaks remaining that haven't been ridden by traveling wave explorers on "surfari." I was lucky enough to make a surf safari to El Salvador in the late 1960s, before their bloody civil war, and earned the distinction of being the third *gringo* to ride these wonderful, isolated waves. My wife, Sarah, was the first woman to surf El Salvador and our son Pahl, at age ten, was certainly the youngest to ride there. We yearn to return to those uncrowded waves and the people who made us feel so welcome.

Australians have been surfing since 1914, when the Duke arrived to show them how. Forty-one years later, a group of young Californians arrived with Malibu boards and their dramatic hotdogging style dazzled the Aussies and the surfing craze exploded Down Under.

In 1956, when 12-year-old Bernard "Midget" Farelly saw those visiting California Yanks ripping up the waves at Manley Beach, he knew with absolute clarity that he had to become a surfer.

The launching of Australia as a world surf power started in 1962 when Farelly won the first Makaha International Surfing Championship riding a Malibu board. Suddenly, to sports-fanatic Aussies, surfing was respectable. Soon two other Aussies entered the scene, Nat Young and Bob McTavish. Young would shortly win a world surfing championship and McTavish, with George Greenough as his mentor, would inspire the shortboard era Down Under. What these three

Aussies and a Yank were really trying to accomplish was total involvement with the wave. Their riding style, when all worked well, achieved a unity between surfer, board, and the wave. As Greenough refined the new boards, these three ripped in the surf. Farelly was the smooth stylist, McTavish the inventor, and Young combined it all by adding his enormous physical power and agility to "new era" Aussie surfing.

Big Changes

Along with the Australians heading full-bore into the surfing scene with their short boards came other changes: soul surfing, big bucks commercialism, professional surf contests, drugs and rock and roll, and media surf heroes.

Television discovered surfing in 1967. Exciting, colorful camera coverage of bronzed wave riders in big Hawaiian surf drew tens of thousands to the waves. In 1967, ABC broadcast the first "Duke" Sunset Beach big wave contest, won by pioneer big wave–surfer Ricky Grigg. I was there with Dr. Don James shooting a photo story for *Life* magazine and the surf cooperated wonderfully. We hired big wave–surfer José Angel to drive our camera boat, the first time anyone was fool or brave enough to work close to the surfers in a boat. Angel was the only waterman then with the skill to pilot our 14-foot Boston whaler in 16- to 20-foot surf without dumping the photographers. We shot 74 rolls of 35mm color film in four hours, and *Life* gave us eight pages and a cover shot on its Spanish-language edition.

Surfers of this pre–Vietnam War era focused on surfing, innovation, travel, bitchin' waves, girls, and supporting themselves so they could keep on surfing. But there was another swell approaching, a big swell that would rise up and shatter the peaceful isolation of surfers from the larger world.

Rolling in from the horizon came the Vietnam War and the counterculture it spawned. Surfers joined the cosmic kids, wore hippie beads, let their hair grow, and embraced peace and love, rock and roll, dope, and soul surfing instead of war. These were the weird times of Woodstock, and surfers, for the most part free-thinkers and social outcasts, were quickly caught up in this mass far-out counterculture. These new-era wave-riders sought a shortcut to spiritual fulfillment and personal expression through the physical high that surfing brought—with a little help from marijuana and other mind-benders.

Surfing trips became expression sessions. The flower children were now slashing the surf instead of flowing with it. Boards became ever shorter, more radical. Draft cards were burned. The big-budget Hollywood, coming-of-age, anti–Vietnam War surfing film *Big Wednesday* reflected a lot of this ferment. While the surf scene bubbled and boiled that pivotal year of 1969, the world changed around the wave-riders. Man walked on the moon, Nixon was losing his sanity, kids by the thousands were dying in Vietnam, the Japanese opened the first artificial wave indoor surfing park, and Gerry Lopez arrived at the Pipeline to surf it better than anyone before, and perhaps since.

Gerry Lopez brought grace and dignity back to surfing. When he emerged on the North Shore surfing scene, that little frenetic world along the Kam Highway was in almost psychotic chaos. Hawaiian, Californian, and Australian factions were ripping apart what unity existed between the international community of surfers. Blame was shotgunned in all directions. Riding out of a huge Pipeline tube came Gerry Lopez, smiling and confident, and he carried his remarkable surfing skill beyond the waves and into the lives of a lot of people who needed a positive role model to emulate. Gerry's gift to surfing was an open Aloha attitude that had room for all and a lot of innovative board designs. His "Lopez Lightning Bolt" surfboards were narrower than most, with sharp pointed noses, an ideal shape for riding fast-breaking Hawaiian surf. The Lightning Bolts led the shortboard design revolution and carried Gary to several victories in Pipeline competitions. These new boards were turned by the forward-facing foot rather than the rear foot used on longboards. Lopez also pioneered surf travels to Indonesia's great waves and Fiji's remarkable Cloudbreak reef, where the first world-class surf camp was built on Tavarua Island. Another of Lopez's contributions was the creation of a cooperative community of board designers, shapers, and surfers who banded together to improve surfing. He also became an important member of the early tow-in surfing group that originated riding huge offshore Hawaiian waves by being towed into about-to-break swells by personal watercraft often known as Jet Skis.

On a surf trip with my wife to Tavarua in 1990 for the first Surfing Medical Association Conference, we piled on an island surf taxi for the ride out to Cloudbreak Reef. As we arrived the wave of the day rolled thunderously over the coral. All but one surfer paddled seaward to escape what looked like a certain closeout. It was Gerry Lopez riding that wave of waves with absolute authority and in true harmony with all that incredible force. Of all the wave riders of the modern era, Lopez could truly be called an icon.

Throughout the 1970s and 1980s surfing contests took off and became big money commercial events, thanks to aggressive sponsors and exciting, hyped-up television coverage. In the surfing world of that era professional contest winners became globetrotting heroes, paid to travel the world. Top professional surfers were earning a $100,000 a year and up from prize money and sponsors. In the eyes of the public and corporate world, surfing had finally arrived as a legitimate professional sport and was ripe to exploit. In California, conservative Congressmen Dana Rohrabacher and Brian Bilbray won re-election by attaching themselves to the surfer image. In Hawaii, pioneer big wave–surfer and former world amateur champion Fred Hemmings ran for lieutenant governor. The slogan on his political poster read, "Hemmings. He doesn't golf." His slight to Hawaii's huge golfing population probably cost him the election.

By 1990 Tom Curren, son of legendary big wave–rider and board builder Pat Curren, was leading the pack of hot pros on tiny tri-fins plastered with advertising stickers that paid their way around the world. Teenage pros and new school freeriders of the early 1990s needed faster, thinner, more responsive boards that could fly. Ever-longer "air time," with spins, loops and barrel rolls prompted development of the pointy, flipped-up nose and wider tail, concave and double concave bottom shapes, with less rocker in the middle of the board.

This remarkable 1953 Makaha big wave photo by Scoop Tsuzuki appeared in hundreds of mainland newspapers and inspired a generation of surfers to migrate to Oahu's North Shore. Dixon Collection

Narrow and thin was in, with basic high-performance small-wave boards now measuring slightly more than six feet long and 18 inches wide.

As the century closed, supreme innovator Kelly Slater ruled contest surfing, with six world championships. And on the other end of the spectrum master stylist Joel Todor from San Clemente dominated the World Longboard Championships on smooth flowing, old school single-fin tankers.

After going through so many phases, 21st-century surfing has come full circle and returned to its roots. There is now full acceptance and respect for any form of wave riding, if done well with a sense of joy and style. Whether the medium is bodysurfing, long- or short-boarding, bodyboarding, wind, kite, tow-in, air mat or whatever, surfers everywhere are rekindling the original pure stoke of simply sliding some waves. Most of us are becoming aware that we are a global tribe with common goals and respect for nature—and deserve communal respect as such. The timeless sport of surfing has grown up to become a gathering of the world's water people. Surfers are part of a planetary subculture based on admiration for our environment and each other as active participants in nature—on her terms. Some of us have become global icons, eco-activists, and even cultural role models for young people. That's an awesome responsibility.

This flowering of aloha and respect for the sport is what all the great surfers strove for. Even Malibu's Surfrider Beach has mellowed and the once-aggressive crowd of surfers is sharing waves. It's up to each of us as surfers to keep the spirit alive by telling the stories of classic surf heroes and villains and helping new wave riders achieve an ocean understanding as they learn about this amazing water world of total freedom in the surf zone.

Which is what riding waves is all about.

Let's Go Surfing

The phone rings, someone stops by your house, friends meet after school or before work. If you live anywhere near the ocean, you'll hear, "Let's go surfing!" or "Surf's up! Let's go for it."

If you're a novice, this invitation may be the beginning of a lifelong adventure. If you've been surfing a while, it's time for another paddle out to the lineup for an enriching experience that challenges your physical skill and leaves you tired and relaxed. There is one gift of surfing on which everyone one who rides waves agrees: "You never worry when you're surfing." You might be concerned about not making a wave or an aggro bozo who's dominating the break, but when you're out in the surf you leave behind the cares and concerns of life on shore.

Surfing is so simple, so essentially pure. Riding a nature-made fun machine is truly one of the great joys of being alive. On a fast-breaking wave, with the peeling shoulder beginning to curl

In a state of balance and grace in the curl of a wave, a surfer practices the ancient sport of royalty.

over you, your senses are absorbed totally in that wet and wild moment. You see, hear, feel, smell everything—even taste the salt.

Every sensation and movement of the wave and ride is transmitted to that part of the brain that gives pleasure. With one exception, surfing has brought me closer than anything to sensing life at its fullest. The only time I've felt more alive, more linked to nature, more fearful, was walking among a pride of twenty-three lions in southern Africa. The nearest vehicle was eight miles away and there was no escape if things went wrong. Fortunately, the lions had fed well the night before.

The few times I've surfed truly big waves, I've had that same feeling of fearful exhilaration. Surfing has also given me moments of profound inner peace. What surfing will do for you will be very personal. It can be mind-expanding, physically rewarding, or simply a lot of fun. It's my hope for you that learning to ride waves will become the first stage of a long journey of excitement and fulfillment.

Let's go.

The Learning Curve

Most beginners want to know how hard it is to learn and how long it will take. As with almost every sport, surfing looks easier than it really is. If you're a beach kid who grew up in the waves, the transition from playful swimmer to stand-up surfer will come as easily as learning to ride a bicycle. If you're in Hawaii and hire a surfing instructor, you can be confidently riding the gentle waves off Waikiki after three or four lessons. The learning curve from total novice to total surfing enjoyment depends upon:

- **Basic athletic ability.** Snow skiers, snowboarders, skateboarders, and competitive swimmers learn to surf faster because of the similarity in physical movements. Strong swimmers, already comfortable in the water, have less fear to overcome, and most learn to surf rapidly. When possible, get lessons from a professional instructor or a surfer friend, who will take the time to teach you and watch out for your safety.

- **The amount of time you practice surfing and paddling.** The more hours spent in the surf the better. If you can surf two or three times a week where the waves are gentle and easy to ride, you'll become a good surfer in a month or even less. If the surf is down and no one is out riding, you can always take a paddle, which is healthy, important practice.

- **How well you can learn from watching other surfers.** The eyes take in great amounts of information that you'll absorb subconsciously. You'll learn more than you think by observing competent surfers. After a few hours of watching waves and surfers you'll know where it's safe to ride, the best route out to the surf, and where to catch a wave. By studying surfers in action you'll learn that once they start sliding down a wave it's important to come to your feet quickly. You'll also see that surfers come in all sizes, and that big bronzed bodies aren't all that important. Some of the most graceful, stylish surfers I've had the privilege to watch are 90-pound women and 250-pound Hawaiians.

Getting Started

To become a surfer, the beginner needs to know something about how and why waves break, basic oceanography, a little about marine life, tides and currents, the effects of weather on surf and sea, and a lot about swimming and watermanship.

Four essentials are required to start: basic sound health, swimming ability, easy surfing waves, and, of course, a proper board to paddle and ride.

If you want to surf, wipeouts are part of the game.

Health

Surfing is a strenuous sport that places great demands on the heart, respiratory system, and muscles. You don't need brute strength to surf, but good health and a body that can be conditioned through training are essential. Older people tend to take more time to get in surfing shape, but that's true for any active sport. Children and teenagers quickly respond to surfing's physical demands, and with a little help are soon catching waves. People with disabilities also surf. The late Bob Simmons, a surfing pioneer and remarkable board designer, had a withered arm. He compensated with determined one-handed paddling. Peter Cole, an all-time Hawaiian North Shore big wave–rider, lost an eye in a surfing accident. His sight was never good, but he kept on riding the heavies.

The one physical prerequisite for surfing is your ability to recover from fatigue. Every time you paddle out, stroke for a wave, then return to paddle out again, you're getting a hard workout. At first, you'll be out of breath and your aching shoulder muscles will cry for a rest. For most people the rest periods become shorter with conditioning and self-confidence in the surf. Gym workouts and jogging will improve your overall physical condition, but there is no substitute for getting in the water and swimming and paddling. After a month of steady surfing, most people will be in great shape and ready to tackle more challenging waves.

Swimming

Swimming well is essential to surfing safely. Despite the almost universal use of board leashes, which allow even poor swimmers to surf, you'll never be safe in the ocean until you become a competent, strong swimmer. This means being able to swim at least a half-mile in rough ocean water and return to the beach without collapsing from exhaustion. A good swimmer need not have a competitive background, though that helps greatly. To swim well requires coaching to learn the various strokes. Swimming laps in a pool, with a coach making corrections, is the easiest way to become water-safe and efficient. Like riding a bicycle, once you've learned to swim well, you'll never forget.

At the pool, practice holding your breath in the deep end, being careful to surface for air well before you're about to black out from lack of oxygen. Don't push it—and have someone watch you. When I swim laps under water, I make sure there's an alert lifeguard keeping an eye on me. When you're comfortable holding your breath for a minute or more, and can swim underwater for a hundred feet, you'll be able to control any panic when held down during a wipeout.

As novice surfers become more skilled, they'll go after bigger waves. Big surf creates its own hazards: hard wipeouts in churning, turbulent water and seaward-flowing ripcurrents. Then there's the danger of being swept into rocks and surf-lashed cliffs. Incidents do occur when it's absolutely necessary to unstrap the surf cord and swim to safety. If you can't swim well, you're a hazard to yourself. And if you do get into an emergency you'll be risking the life of the person attempting to save you.

Waves

To be a surfer, you have to be where the swells feel the drag of the bottom, rise up, then overbalance to become ridable waves. No waves, no surfing. Sure, there are artificial, machine-made waves at dozens of water parks. People do surf boat wakes, tidal bores, and standing waves found on rivers. If pure, nature-made ocean waves are what you want to surf, you'll have to make the commitment to be where they are, because the real thing doesn't happen at water theme parks, lakes, or rivers.

Though these Malibu waves are crowded, they're still fun to ride. Dixon photo

Really, there are waves of some sort to ride, if the water's not polluted, off every coastline in the world. Years back, surfing was California, Australia, and Hawaii. Today, surfers are riding waves off Alaska, in the winter surf off Maine, and among icebergs in the Antarctic.

A beginner would be wise to avoid crowded surf spots. If the waves are jammed with other surfers, you'll have little chance catching a ride. It's very discouraging to paddle into the crowd and be greeted with cold indifference, or at some breaks, with open hostility. Look for an area with small, gentle waves no more than two to three feet high that spill from top to bottom.

Avoid beaches where the surf batters rocks. If you can see one rock jutting from the water, know there are more out of sight underwater. Just paddling a board in small waves and riding the white water lying flat on the board will be fun. The more you're in the water, the more you'll learn what surfing is all about. And please, don't paddle out in surf beyond your capability. Starting out in pounding shorebreak, where waves rise up and dump violently close to the beach, is hazardous. These hard-crashing waves are called *sandbusters*, and for good reason. Beaches that drop off quickly to deep, over-the-head water usually produce pounding shorebreak. Stay in small surf when starting out. Trying to paddle out through big wet avalanches of churning white water and being washed back to the beach again and again is discouraging as well as dangerous. When the surf looks gnarly and makes you feel uneasy, listen to that inner voice of caution and stay on the beach.

Your First Surfboard

As I started to write this, a question came to mind: "How does a surfboard work?"

In all the years I've surfed, this question never occurred to me. It took some thinking to realize a surfboard is really a thin, buoyant, flat-bottomed boat with a pointed bow and tapered stern. The board's long, graceful shape allows it to glide *over* the water rather than plow *through* it. When you paddle a surfboard onto the unbroken face of a steep wave, gravity takes over and the board begins a downward slide. As long as the wave's slope keeps moving shoreward and the wave face remains steep enough, the board will continue moving. When we learn to stand on a board's deck and control its direction, we can harness the power of a wave.

Board Types

Most any kind of old surfboard that's buoyant enough to float you will do for paddling and getting in shape, but choosing the right board to begin riding waves takes some care. Surfboards are constantly evolving, yet never perfected. When deciding on a first board, ask yourself how you want to surf. Want to glide and slide for recreation, or go for big waves? Are you quick and fit enough to master a shortboard? Are you a big person who needs the extra floatation of a long buoyant surfboard or a lightweight better suited for a smaller one?

Before starting out, it's important to gain an understanding of basic surfboard shapes and how they perform. Then you can select a board that will make learning easier.

Surfboards have evolved into three basic types:

- The traditional longboard, with a rounded nose, straight midsection and wide tail. Longboards are defined more by shape than by length. A longboard can be eight feet or twelve feet, as long as it's shaped more like a tongue depressor than a tuna fish. Longboards have one fin, which is attached to the board's underside near its tail. (Fins are sometimes called "skegs." When hit by a fin, you've

Hot competitive surfer Jay Moriarity demonstrates how versatile a longboard can be in skilled hands.

been "skegged.") For the beginner the only sensible choice is a longboard.

- The narrow, pointed-nose shortboard. Shortboards are thin and streamlined, with an abrupt rise in the nose, called the *kick*. They can be five feet, six inches or longer and are not very buoyant. Shortboards usually have three fins.

- Various hybrids that combine elements of both longboards and shortboards. Hybrids take many forms and are commonly called funboards.

Longboards

A well-shaped longboard will provide an effortless glide across a wave that is aesthetically appealing and wonderful.

Developed in the 1950s, the easy-riding longboard inspired the surfing craze of the 1960s. These lighter-weight boards were easier to paddle than the traditional boards developed in Hawaii, and they made surfing accessible to the average person. Women could now

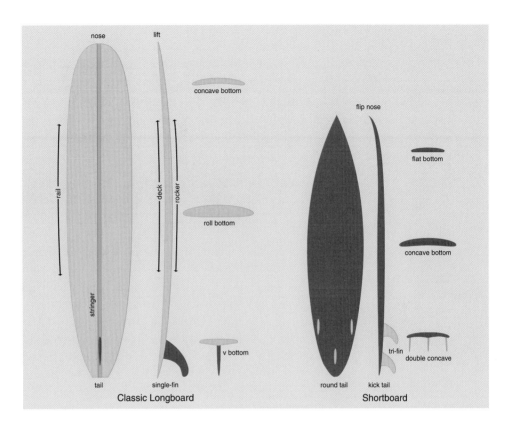

Surfboard anatomy.

carry a balsa board with ease and join the men in the surf. The classic longboard, which had one huge fin, very little nose or tail kick, and round edges, or *rails*, from nose to tail, was ten feet long, two feet wide, four inches thick, and weighed about thirty-five pounds, as opposed to the historical one hundred-pound-plus, sixteen-foot Hawaiian boards, which had no fins.

Today's longboards still mimic the original design concept. They're easy to paddle, glide effortlessly on small waves, and provide a stable platform for turns, cutbacks, nose rides and other basic maneuvers. Over the past two decades longboards have shed 20 pounds, lost a bit of thickness, and can be any length from eight feet to as long as 12 feet for real heavyweights.

By incorporating many of the shortboard's features, today's longboards are much easier to ride than the old logs and have made surfing more accessible than ever. Design variations include soft, foam-coated longboards for beginners and Sunday surfers. Soft boards are a good option for the beginner before moving up to a hard longboard. Surfboard shops often sell used softboards with the understanding that the customer can trade it in when moving up to a conventional surfboard.

Riding a longboard allows a surfer to hold that wonderful erect posture while gliding across a perfect, glassy wave. Longboard riding is more relaxed, and the people who ride them seem more willing to share the waves.

When selecting a longboard, the beginners should consider the following:

- *Can you carry it? Does it fit under your arm?* Your fingers should be able to curl around the board's rail so you'll have a firm grip when climbing down and back that steep trail to the beach.
- *Could you carry it a mile?* If you're hiking in to an isolated beach, you might have to carry the board a long ways.
- *Is it buoyant enough to support your weight?* It's harder to paddle a "sinker." A board that's easy to paddle is a safer board.
- *Will it be suitable for where you'll surf the most?* A small, unstable board is just not safe in big surf. And a 10-foot tanker is overkill in small waves unless you're a heavyweight. Size and buoyancy are important considerations.

Here are some basic guidelines on suggested longboard dimensions as they relate to a surfer's weight:

Rider Weight	Board Size
50 lbs	7' x 20" x 2"
100 lbs	8' x 21" x 2.5"
150 lbs	9' x 22" x 3"
200 lbs	10' x 23" x 3.5"
250 lbs	11' x 24" x 4"

The suggested dimensions above are for the average beginning surfer who wants a fun and easy experience on a board that floats under load, paddles well, and is easy to ride in small to medium surf.

Other Features

From above, the board's nose and tail should appear balanced, with neither end wider or thicker than the other. Thick boards are more

These scale models depict the evolution of the modern surfboard over the past hundred years. The diorama of Dana Point, a quality California surfing break destroyed by a harbor development, is a reminder of what can happen if surfers don't take a stand to protect the ocean and their sport. Courtesy: Malcolm Wilson

buoyant and easier to paddle, but are usually a bit slower in the wave. The average modern longboard has a thickness of 3½ inches. Anything over four inches is too thick for an average sized surfer.

From the side, check the board's *foil*, which refers to the combination of its thickness and *rocker*, the amount of curve along its length (think of a rocking chair). The rocker should be relatively uniform, with neither end of the board more than two inches out from the other. A board's rocker is important. Look for a board with a small amount of rocker. Avoid "banana rocker" boards that have excessive midsection curvature, because these boards push water instead of gliding.

The sharper curvature at the nose and tail is called *kick*. More nose kick helps prevent *pearling*, an unfortunate mishap caused by the nose of the board digging in and abruptly slowing down. When you pearl on takeoff, the board's nose drives deep underwater, the board stops abruptly, and you fly off. But as with cars, boats, build-

A skilled longboard surfer can handle even this critical, about-to-break wave.

ings, or just about anything else, surfboard design is a series of compromises. It's true that more nose kick will help you avoid pearling, but it also slows down the board and interferes with nose riding. More tail kick makes turning easier, but also slows down the board a bit in fast surf.

Avoid longboards that are flat across the bottom and middle in cross-section. From side to side, the board's bottom should be slightly rounded to prevent the edges from digging in (*catching*) and toppling the surfer. The underside of the tail area should have a slight 1/8-inch to 1/4-inch V that peaks at the leading edge of the fin. The bottom of the nose area should be flat across or even slightly concave for easier nose riding.

Basic longboard rails should be rounded at the outer edge, with a slight lip underneath to release unwanted drag that forms from water wrapping around the deck. Fully rounded rails cause drag; super-sharp rails go fast, but tend to catch on choppy water and cause the board to spin out. For the average surfer who rides medium-size waves, medium-thick rounded rails with a mild tuck edge underneath usually work best.

A New or Used Board?

If you can afford a new board, decide what you need and buy one off a shop rack. New boards are expensive and could set you back as much as $400. You could have a board custom made, but it will take a month or more before it's in your hands. Occasionally, custom boards don't arrive as ordered. When you select a factory-made board off the rack, you'll at least get what you see. Most surf shops will happily assist you in selecting the right size and shape for your build and ability. Don't be concerned about admitting you're a novice: everyone was at one point. Friends who surf will also offer advice on choosing your first board, but consider that their opinion could be based on personal preference and not what you actually need to start. And remember that you don't have to buy the first board that's offered. Shop around. Listen to the salespeople. Find someone to talk with who has been around the surfing retail game for a while. Their advice is usually sound. They want you to come back for your second or third board.

Used boards range from pristine, almost-new models without a ding or scratch, to really thrashed, water-logged tankers that have seen much

Shortboard surfers mix it up. Note diamond-shaped nose guard on the younger surfer's board.

better days. Used boards in near perfect shape sell at close to the price of a new one. The compromise is to find a board that's reasonably free of patched-over wounds, stains from water that has seeped under the fiberglass covering, and signs of major repairs. There should be no cracks in the glass around the fins, nose, and tail. Look for dents in the deck that could indicate deteriorating foam underneath the fiberglass. A board that has been painted may cover defects you don't want to deal with. Most surf shops won't sell junk. They may charge more than that "used board for sale" ad in a recycler newspaper, but you'll be getting a better surfboard. Expect to pay at least $150 to $200 for a clean, ding-free used board.

Before You Go Out—Mastering the Basics

The first step in learning to surf is watching others surf, *really* watching what they do. As mentioned earlier, your eye and mind can take in a tremendous amount of information, shift it about, and allow you to imitate the experts. Watch where they place themselves in relation to the wave and you'll learn the best spot to catch one. Notice where and

Surfing instructor Nancy Emerson has a new surfer practice on the sand before paddling out.

how they paddle out and you'll understand the easiest way to reach the break. There's a reason for almost every move in surfing. "Watching" should also include renting surf videos and studying how the experts catch waves and handle demanding surf.

If possible, put yourself in the care of an experienced surfing instructor. The expense of a few professional lessons will save weeks of frustration, and you'll have someone who will explain the rules of the waves and a lot more. Pick up one of the several surfing magazines (see Resources, page 191) to check out surfing schools, camps, and instructors. Your next best choice is a patient friend who surfs well—a friend won't let you go out in waves you aren't prepared for.

Preliminaries

Wetsuit. Where the water's chilly, you'll need a wetsuit. Paddling out for the first time in cold water just isn't fun. A wetsuit gives a certain feeling of security and the water that seeps in around your neck, wrists, and ankles will soon warm from body heat. You'll find a discussion on wetsuits in chapter 6, Gear.

Wax. Before paddling out you'll notice that every surfer waxes his board. This little dollar bar of tacky stuff that's rubbed on the top deck of

Starting at an early age with mom or dad as teacher is the best way to learn to surf.

the board helps keep your feet and body from slipping off the slick fiberglass surface. Without the traction surf wax provides, we'd fall off the board the first time we push a foot down to turn away from the break. Waxing is a must before a "go-out." Rub on a thick coat of wax before paddling out. We'll go into the technique and ritual of waxing in chapter 6.

Leash. The surf leash should always be checked prior to going out. Make sure the Velcro strap between the cord and where it's attached to the board is securely fastened. If the strap comes free during a wipeout you'll lose you're board and have to swim after it. The board will usually reach the beach before you can grab it, unless it shatters itself on the rocks or smacks a little kid in the ankles. You could really be unlucky and find that your bouncing board takes out a personal injury lawyer.

Most surfers attach the ankle end of the leash just above the foot that faces the rear of the surfboard. This helps keep the strap away from the other leg and reduces the chance of it tangling around your feet. The Velcro closure should be just tight enough so the strap can move freely around the ankle. On the beach, practice freeing the leash a few times so you'll get the feel of how it comes off if you need to disconnect yourself in the water. Leashes do get tangled in floating seaweed or around rocks. It's a good idea to keep an eye on the strap in case it becomes tangled.

Paddling

Paddling is as much a part of surfing as catching a wave. Paddling well will increase your safety in the surf and allow you to catch more waves. There's no way you'll surf well without learning to paddle efficiently. Paddling out to the break takes effort; but the more one practices paddling, the easier it becomes.

The secret to paddling well lies in proper board balance and stroke technique. On stable longboards, surfers can paddle either in the prone or kneeling position. Because shortboards are tippy and lack buoyancy, the only way to paddle them is prone. In days gone by, the standard paddling technique called for both arms pulling through the water at once, a method still used when knee paddling. Today, most surfers paddle prone using a crawl stroke, alternating pulling with each arm.

Body position on the board is crucial to good paddling. If you're too far forward, the nose of the board digs in and you'll take water in your face. Too far back and the board's tail drags, making paddling harder. Get back just far enough from the center to bring the nose of the board an inch or two above water, so it doesn't plow in. If the surf is choppy, keep the nose higher by moving back slightly so it won't catch water. Lie or kneel over the board's centerline. If you're leaning even slightly to the side, the board will tip and over you'll go. After a few paddling sessions, a balanced position comes naturally.

Head up, back arched—great paddling form.

When prone paddling keep your head up and back slightly arched. This allows arm, back, and shoulder muscles to work in concert. When all these muscles are working together, you'll feel the board gliding almost effortlessly. Watch how experienced surfers paddle and imitate them. On a long paddle, alternate between prone and knee paddling to give the different muscle groups a bit of a rest. Knee paddling requires more attention to balance, but if the board is stable that position comes easily.

One tip on learning to knee paddle: start out by paddling prone. Once the board has gained momentum, rise to your knees and take a few hard strokes to stabilize yourself. Most knee paddlers sit on their heels between strokes and then rock forward to take the next stroke. On the takeoff the kneeling position allows the surfer to come to his or her feet a bit quicker.

Once you're comfortable paddling straight ahead you can work on turning. You can make slight turns by leaning in the direction you want to go. Some surfers drag a foot, like a rudder, which helps turn the board. Right foot in, turn right; left foot, turn left. You can make an abrupt 180-degree turn by sitting near the tail of the board and raising the nose high out of the water. Then, arm strokes and counter-rotating leg kicks will pivot the board. Most surfers face out to sea while waiting for a wave and spin quickly as it rises. As the board comes around they throw their weight forward and paddle hard down the face of the wave. If the timing is correct, and the wave close to breaking, a one-stroke takeoff results—and that's a great feeling.

Paddling can be a sport in itself. Paddleboards have been in use as long as surfboards. Paddling competitions go back to pre-European Hawaii. Lifeguards use oversized longboards for rescues and ultra-sleek, low-weight racing paddleboards for ocean competition can be as long as sixteen feet. Champion paddlers can stroke for hours and a twenty-mile race is only a warm-up for a well-trained waterman.

Getting to Your Feet

Mastering paddling is just the first step along your path to that first successful ride. Learning to spring quickly to your feet at the start of your slide is essential. Try it first by practicing on the beach. Lie on top of the board and spring up from a pushup position while at the same time drawing your legs beneath your body in a single fluid movement. Without hesitating, or coming to your knees first, you take a crouched stance on the centerline of the board. You'll be standing sideways, knees bent, with your feet at right angles to the board's centerline. Of course you can practice this again and again by yourself until standing flows naturally, as it will with time.

Practicing coming to your feet will let you know if your normal surfing stance is "regular" or "goofy" foot. Being "regular" means that your left foot will be forward of the right when your come to your feet. This is as natural as being left- or right-handed. Your body will tell you which is more comfortable for you. Some surfers can switch stances easily. Regular foot surfers tend to surf better going right because it places their backs to the wave. The reverse is true for goofy footers, who usually prefer going to the left. It's a good idea to practice both stances so you can comfortably surf right or left breaking waves.

Your First Ride

We've checked off the prelims, have a good grip on paddling proficiently, and have practiced springing to our feet quickly and fluidly. Now it's time to get wet and slide that first wave. Today the surf is small and spilling shoreward, and the sea surface smooth, almost glassy: perfect conditions for a beginner. An experienced friend is along for the ride and offers constant advice: "We'll go out here. No rocks. Notice that the waves are in sets of three to five today. We'll paddle out between sets and ride in on the white water. No sweat. It's really small today."

"What happens if a wave comes when we're paddling out?"

"Paddle harder and punch through."

Big waves or small, surfing's always an exciting challenge.

When you wade out, remember to point the board into the surf. In waist-deep water a small wave rolls in. You're watching the surfers in the lineup and allow the board to turn sideways. Now the board is parallel to the beach instead of pointing into the surf. The small wave, you, and the board meet. The board takes its full force, becomes a battering ram and smashes into your stomach. Luckily, the wave had no real power and it only knocks you down. Your friend laughs and remarks, "Sorry, I forgot to mention that you always keep the board pointed into the wave."

Since you've paddled several times for practice, it's no big deal to get out beyond the small shore-rushing whitewater. You turn the board to face shore and your friend says, "Take the first one prone, so you'll get the feeling of the takeoff and slide. And, once you start sliding, shift your weight back just enough to keep the nose from digging in . . . that's called pearling."

Minutes later he points out to sea and nods. Rolling in comes an already broken wave with a face of tumbling white water. Your friend yells encouragement, "A couple good strokes and you've got it!"

He's right. Three strokes starts you for the beach. Then the white water (often called soup) overtakes the board. You're caught up in the tumbling, splashing water and carried shoreward. For several brief, all-too-short seconds you're surfing. Then the nose digs in and the wave sweeps you off the board. Your mentor has you practice riding the soup again and again. Now he says, "On the next one, come to your knees." You do and it's easy. He has you turn a bit by leaning slightly left and right. Gaining confidence, you stand on the next wave and promptly fall off. It's shallow. You hit the bottom. The board washes on until the leash snaps it back, and it whacks your leg.

Your friend suggests enough for one day. You shake your head, "Hey, I'm just getting started."

"Okay! Let's paddle out to the lineup."

Paddling Out

There's no reason to waste energy fighting through breaking surf when in a few minutes the waves will diminish and there will be a period of calm. You've been watching the sets and where other surfers have paddled out, so it's a no-brainer to reach the lineup. Since the surf is small, only a few others are out to compete for the mellow waves.

You and your friend hang back, waiting a turn to take off just beyond where the waves are breaking. You're a non-local here and the most acknowledgment you get is a brief nod. When everyone has caught several waves, and you're growing frustrated and impatient, someone finally says, "Okay, your turn. Go for it!"

In comes a small wave with clean breaking shoulder. You decide it's yours and start paddling. The others hoot encouragement. You paddle harder. Suddenly the tail of the board lifts, the nose points downward, and the board begins to slide on its own. You're surfing. Now the big move, the one you practiced again and again on the beach. You come to your feet in a smooth flowing motion. As you stand, you plant your feet wide apart for good balance, at almost a right angle to its center-line. If the takeoff angle "feels" extra steep you'll want to be standing behind the board's midpoint. If the wave is shallow you'll move forward to keep the nose down to prevent stalling out of the wave. Surfing down the wave's face, your senses tell you that its breaking shoulder is coming closer and closer. From watching other surfers, you intuitively, almost unconsciously, push down the back of the board with your rear foot. The board responds by turning away from the wave's breaking shoulder. The sensation of speed and exhilaration is breathtaking. You take a quick glance over the top of the wave to see if your friend is watching. Not a good idea to distract yourself. The nose goes down and digs in. Next the tail comes up and the inrushing wave flips the board over. You fly off to be buried in a cascade of whitewater and experience an easy first wipeout—a baptism all surfers go through repeatedly.

Though fictional and idealized, that was a very good first day of basics for a beginner. In chapter 4 we'll go into detail about what's needed to really get started and move on to intermediate surfing skills the right way, the fun way, and the safe way.

Next, let's learn more about the waves that make surfing possible. Without an understanding of how they form, break, and become ridable you won't become a skilled and safe surfer.

A wet-and-wild wipeout.

CHAPTER
··· Three ···

Waves

The waves we ride today were generated days ago and thousands of miles away. A basic understanding of the dynamics of how ocean swells become waves will help any surfer appreciate the complexity of something so simple and beautiful as a breaking wave. With increased understanding of why ocean swells rise to become surf, you'll be better able to recognize the oceans' moods and catch more waves. Her moods are important. An angry sea is not forgiving.

For thousands of years, seafarers have known that waves are born from the mating of wind-blown ripples across the sea's surface. Only in recent times, however, have oceanographers discovered how complex the process of wave formation is. Changes in barometric pressure, depth of water, bottom topography, and the push of winds blowing from multiple directions all affect waves and how they break when reaching shore.

Before a wave sends a surfer sliding shoreward the wind must meet three basic requirements. It must:

Closeout wave, The Pipeline. Note wave tube exploding out of the left. Dixon photo

1) Blow over the water with sufficient velocity to start the surface of the sea in motion.

2) Blow for a sufficient length of time in a constant direction, and

3) Blow over a long distance of open water.

For surfing waves to form the minimum distance is roughly 800 miles. The longer the winds blow, the farther the swells travel, and the bigger and better the surf becomes. When all these conditions come to-gether for several days, enormous open-ocean swells occur. As these heaving monsters reach land it's glory time for big wave–surfers—or a day to stay out of the water for most of us.

Later we'll discuss how nearshore bottom topography affects wave size and shape—and how this relates to catching a ride. First, though, let's define wave size in terms that surfers generally use, so you'll understand when you hear an excited surfer say, "Hey, it's overhead at Rincon!"

Surf size is usually measured from the trough, or bottom of the wave front, which is often called the *face*. Surf size, and how local surfers perceive the incoming swells, varies a great deal from beach to beach. Big surf at Malibu might be in the six-foot range. In Hawaii, surf isn't called big by the locals until it climbs to 12 feet high. For a new surfer a three-foot foot wave may seem huge. A big wave–rider wouldn't be concerned until the surf became 20 feet high.

Here's a very subjective description of wave size:

- *Small surf* is one to two feet high. Because smaller waves have less power they're easier to paddle out through and catch. Beginners should learn in small surf.

- *Medium surf* ranges from three to five feet high and usually presents little in the way of hazards. These are fun-size waves that most surfers ride. With increased wave height comes an increase in force and speed, which requires more skill.

- *Big surf* means waves of six to eight feet high for the average surfer along the East and West Coasts of North America. Waves of this size have real power and can lead to harder wipeouts. Big surf is for the experienced only.

- *Overhead and double-overhead waves.* When surfers say, "It's overhead," they mean the wave height is actually over the rider's head when surfing in. If a six-footer happily says, "I caught a double-overheader today," it means he was surfing 12-foot waves.

- *Giant surf.* This means waves of 15 or 16 feet and up. Here the equation of size, mass, steepness and speed all come together to produce awesome forces. Add ripcurrents, rocks and reefs, cold water, out-of-control surfers and their flailing boards, and you have truly dangerous conditions. For the expert waterman or waterwoman only.

The Birth of a Wave

The world's oceans extend thousands of miles between the coasts of major landmasses. These long stretches of open water enable the energy of the wind to be transmitted to the sea. The ocean swells that create the waves that break on your local beach were born with the first gentle brush of wind across water. The wind gives rise to ruffled patches that grow into small wavelets. As the speed of this new wave increases, it combines with other smaller waves and becomes increasingly more symmetrical: a true ocean swell. On the open ocean this interaction between wind and water can produce swells that could rise as high as 100 feet, though this is exceptional. These swells will ultimately reach shore and feel the drag of a bottom. When they do slow down, the swells become waves that rise to pitch forward, and we have surf that sends us riding shoreward.

Approaching swells seen from the beach, especially large ones, appear to be line after line of advancing, moving water. In fact, the water itself is not moving, but rather it is the wave moving through the water. It only appears that the water is moving toward you. (If these often huge walls of water did roll forward, the low lying coastal areas of the world would be inundated—as happens when a true tidal wave, a *tsunami*, strikes.) Watch some seaweed or driftwood floating on the surface. When a swell passes through, the object moves up and down, but only slightly forward.

Surf

When swells meet the shore, or anything that obstructs their movement, they lose energy and begin to change shape. As a swell rushes into shallow water, its lower part feels the drag, or friction, of the shore bottom. Since the water closest to the bottom is slowed first, swells begin to rise and pitch forward. When swells become so steep that they no longer can hold their form, the crests topple into the trough and we have a wave. If the shape and size are right for surfing, someone will eventually paddle out and ride the break.

Waves start breaking when the depth of the water is approximately one and one-third of the waves' height. For example, a three-foot wave will break in about four feet of water and a nine foot wave will rise up to break in a depth of 12 feet. Since no two waves are ever alike, nor do they reach shore in precise, orderly rows this rule of thumb is inexact, but it does provide a basis for estimates. Remember also that this is the normal pattern for surf at a normal beach. As every surfer knows, waves don't always behave normally. Add offshore winds to hold the wave face up and it breaks closer to shore than the rule suggests. Some waves will break in water twice their depth, others will suck out and reveal a dry, gnarly reef.

With weather satellites transmitting real-time data, the surfing public now has access to forecasts that can be quite accurate. Major swells can be predicted a week in advance. Winter swells generated by storms off Alaska that bombard Hawaii's North Shore travel thousands of miles before feeling the reefs below the Pipeline, Makaha, or Sunset Beach. In summer, California's big surf comes from storm winds blowing across the southern oceans as far away as the Tasman Sea off Australia. Puerto Rico's western beaches receive great surf from consistent winds blowing across the Caribbean all the way from the Texas coast. On the North American Atlantic coast, waves usually don't have time to develop fully because Atlantic storms tend to occur closer to shore. Yet, the swells that reach the surfing beaches of western France come rolling in with graceful precision.

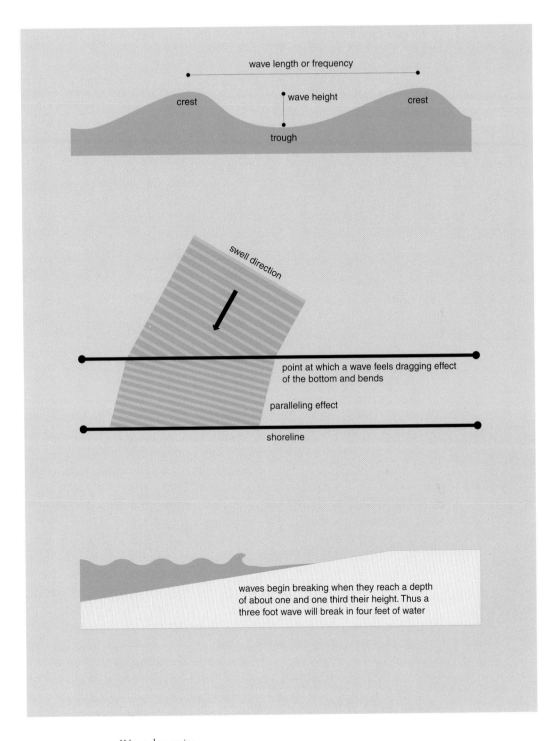

Wave dynamics.

The Big Ones

The distance a wave travels from its creation by the wind to its breakup on shore is called its *fetch*. A wave's highest point is its *crest* and its lowest the *trough*. Waves are also said to have length, which is defined as the distance between crests. The longer the *wavelength*, the more energy a wave can absorb from the wind and the higher the swell will grow. That's why a swell's fetch is so important in predicting wave size. Generally, a fetch of 600 to 800 miles is needed to produce waves high enough to surf.

Surfers talk endlessly about giant waves and incredible triple overhead surf. Old-timers are especially prone to recount epic rides to younger wave riders. Stories usually begin . . . *"Yeah, it was the big winter swell of '69. The whole North Shore was closed out, but me and Buzzy decided we could get out at . . ."* Some of these tall wave tales are true and some of them grow with time.

Here's a true big-wave story that's hard to beat. The amazing account was documented in the *Proceedings of the U.S. Naval Institute* and in Rachel Carson's pioneering must-read book, *The Sea Around Us*. A U.S. Navy oil tanker, the USS *Ramapo*, was outbound from Manila enroute to San Diego in the winter of 1933. The tanker's captain, Lt. Commander R.

Lines of ground swells, soon to become huge waves, are about to close out on these surfers and bodyboarders.

P. Whitemarsh, had anxiously watched severe storm conditions develop for several days. In the ship's log he recorded persistent winds of 30 to 50 knots blowing day and night. The barometer began falling and almost hit bottom at 29.20 inches. As the winds continued to blow, giant swells came rolling for the ship's stern, threatening to swamp her. Luckily the *Ramapo* was a big 478-foot-long tanker and took the swells steadily. At the height of the storm one of the bridge lookouts glanced astern and saw a tremendous wave overtaking them. As the wave overtook the ship its stern rose steeply and its bow sank deep into the trough. To the lookout's horrified surprise, the swell climbed higher than the ship's crow's nest. Looming over the tanker, the huge monster swell threatened to break. Fortunately it didn't pitch over and passed the ship by. Later, with the aid of simple geometry, the captain calculated that the wave was at least 112 feet high. Its speed was estimated at 55 knots.

Can any of the Hawaiian big-wave personal watercraft–assisted tow-in surfers top this? Would anyone want to? Maybe Ken Bradshaw and the North Shore crew of tow-in big-wave riders. On the ultimate "Big Wednesday" of 1998, Bradshaw was towed into an epic 80-foot wave at Outside Log Cabins by his Jet-Ski–driving surfing partner, Dan Moore. Everything came together for Bradshaw and Moore, and Bradshaw successfully surfed what is considered to be the biggest wave ever ridden so far.

These two tow-in surfers knew that swell conditions would be perfect for their attempt to ride the largest waves ever attempted. They had advanced warning from the U.S. Weather Bureau in Honolulu and its prediction of giant swells was correct. Surfers can also get forecasts of wave conditions, and a lot of other information, from the Internet at www.surfline.com or www.swell.com.

Bottom Contour and Wave Shape

After a big day at Cloudbreak, Tavarua, Fiji, I wrote, "We stared at the giant, storm-born swells rolling in from the southern seas, and sensed they were growing ever larger. The swells, which would soon become ridable surf (if we dared) marched in relentlessly, felt the drag of bottom, and began to slow. That friction of water against jagged coral caused the massive undulating humps to rise up, over-balance, and pitch viciously forward. For an instant before they broke and became tumbling surf, the crests hovered as if not wanting to end their long journey. Then each wave broke and spilled, rumbling downward to destroy itself in a white-maned explosion on this remote Fijian reef."

Those Cloudbreak waves were truly awesome. On that day we were facing an onslaught of no-holds-barred killer surf, one of nature's

These huge reef-breaking Pipeline tubes look a bit much for the bodyboard crew waiting to paddle out.

most powerful forces. Knowing my limitations, I stayed in the surf taxi and shot pictures.

Bottom contour is especially important in producing quality surfing waves. For surfers, three types of wave breaks hold special interest: reef break, point break, and sandbar/shore break. Of course, these features might combine to produce point break with sandbars, for example. These varying bottom contours produce waves that either pitch violently from top to bottom, or roll downward from the crest. Bottom and shore contour will greatly influence the shape a surfable wave takes. Good examples of rolling or gently-spilling surf can be found at Waikiki, where long swells break smoothly from the top and roll forward over a gradually shallowing bottom. On the other side of Oahu, the Pipeline, a reef break, has a steeply angled bottom profile which produces dynamic tubing waves.

Point Break

Point surf is the easiest for beginners to learn in. Surfers search the world for perfect point breaks, which are special because they create

California's premier point break, Surfrider Beach, Malibu. Even in the mid 1960s, when this historic photo was taken, the waves were crowded. Photo: Dick Gustafson from Peter Dixon Collection

surf that peels off a landmass projecting into the sea. When swells encounter a point they're bent, or refracted, shoreward as they advance into shallow water. This refraction is akin to light passing through a denser medium such as glass or water. The refraction of swells causes them to draw more closely to shore, and the waves' speed is reduced. Again, the friction of the bottom causes the wave to rise up, overbalance, and become surf. The degree of bottom slope and the shape of the point all influence the final shape a point wave will take.

Surfrider Beach at Malibu, and Makaha Beach on Oahu are two famous examples of point breaks. Surfrider also has a gradually ascending rocky reef off its point to help keep the waves peeling. At Malibu the headland causes the incoming summer south swells to refract. Combine this with a reef-like bottom profile that ascends gradually and conditions are ideal for well-formed waves that roll in for a considerable distance. Rides of a quarter mile are common at Malibu, and some waves can support several riders at once.

Even a small projection of land easing seaward into advancing swells will help form surfable waves. Most points will produce surf even if the swells are small. Malibu is ridable from one foot and up. Piers, jetties, rock outcroppings, and even the hull of a beached ship will refract swells, causing them to crest and become surf. Point surf will only break so far offshore, allowing surfers to paddle around the impact zone instead of having to fight through the whitewater.

Reef Break

Reef breaks produce some of the most exciting surfing areas known. Think of Sunset Beach and the Pipeline in Hawaii, San Onofre, Wind and Sea, giant waves Mavericks in California, and Tavarua's Cloudbreak in Fiji—all world-renowned reef breaks. Surfing a reef break has certain advantages. Usually there is deep water between the reef and shore that will cushion a wipeout, depending on local underwater topography and tide level. The deeper water inside a reef keeps the surf from collapsing suddenly and helps produce longer rides. Add a deep-water channel to either side of a reef, like at Cloudbreak, and the wave will form a shoulder that holds for exceptionally long rides. Where

The steeply shallowing coral reef bottom off the North Shore consistently produces some of the best surf in the world.

these channels are especially deep the wave will flatten, giving the surfer a wave-free route to paddle out. If the reef has a channel on either end, or a depression in the center, it will form a wave with shoulders, allowing right or left slides.

Add a change in the swell size and direction, the tide, and wind angle, and the surfing spot that was so great suddenly becomes impossible to ride. Think of it this way. Some reefs lie in shallow water, others in deep water. Shallow-water reefs will cause swells to become surf in lesser depths, which means smaller waves will break over the reef. A deep-water reef won't show surf until swells arrive to drag on its bottom and become surf.

I don't recommend surfing Cloudbreak, or most nearshore reef breaks, at low tide when the inside reef becomes visible. One day at low tide, I was riding six-foot waves when I wiped out at Cloudbreak and was swept over the jagged coral. The board took most of the thrashing until my leash snagged on a coral head, pulling me off. The whitewater still had some force and the coral did its work on my legs. By then I was so far inside it took an exhausting half hour to paddle back to the break. Other deep-water reef breaks require a low tide for the waves to form.

With experience, all these wave variables can be computed into an accurate prediction of what kind of surf to expect at a certain location. It also helps to have a local surfer along who knows the reef and what conditions make for good waves. If the local fishermen say it's shark waters, believe them and stay on shore. If there's a beach lifeguard on duty, feel free to ask about surf conditions, hazards, or where to find a good hamburger. It's their job to know.

Shore and Sandbar Breaks

Shorebreak is what the name implies, waves that break close to the beach. During the era of long wooden boards and straight-ahead surfing styles, riding shorebreak was almost impossible, and if attempted, downright dangerous. Surfers back then just couldn't turn those old long boards fast enough to avoid a crunching wipeout. Today's highly maneuverable shortboards make riding shorebreak possible and have opened up a whole new surfing style. Surfers can safely take off in a fast-collapsing wave with some assurance they'll get a quick ride before the wave closes out. Most of the surfing done on the Atlantic coast is off shorebreaks, except where points start waves forming such as Point Judith, Rhode Island.

There's a difference between surfable shorebreak and sand-busting crashers. Shorebreak waves hold a face long enough for a quick, fast ride. It's my opinion that the majority of surfing accidents occur when beginners attempt to ride waves that break very quickly close to shore.

59

Pounding shore break, North Shore, Oahu. Bones would be broken, or worse, in that surf.

If you see the wave crashing only yards out from dry sand, and can hear it thumping, it's a dangerous shorebreaker. Beaches that drop off sharply into over-the-head depths almost always have close to shore, hard-breaking waves.

I cringe when some enthusiastic novice paddles for a top to bottom instantaneously breaking sand buster. Being a former beach lifeguard, I often start to run for the water in case the unknowing beginner does a head plant in the sand and needs rescuing. Again and again, safety in the surf depends on knowing what the hazards are.

Beaches with rideable shorebreak have a gradually descending bottom. The degree of slope must be gentle enough to create a spilling wave rather than a crasher. So look for a wave that rises up, falls forward from its crest and rolls on. The direction of swell and bottom contours greatly influence how shorebreak waves will form. Look for waves with shoulder. No matter how quickly they show and then vanish, it's best to take off where there's a shoulder and a momentary chance of turning away from the break. Most times beach breaking waves will have a certain spot where shoulders occur. Look for that spot, or watch where the locals are catching waves. A final caution: shorebreak surfing is exciting and fast moving. Wipeouts happen with split-second speed and the hard bottom is always there. Riding shorebreak is not for the beginner, but as you gain experience it can be a thrilling part of surfing.

Sandbars come and go with a frustrating fickleness. Sandbars build as currents move huge volumes of sand about and deposit it seemingly at random. Within hours, a wonderful break off a sandy beach, with ridable left and right shoulders, could be obliterated as currents sweep the sand elsewhere.

On the East Coast of the United States, sandbars often build offshore. Between the break and beach lies an area of deeper water. If the Atlantic swells are large and consistent, and the water deep enough, good surf builds as swells cross these bars. These conditions exist almost anywhere there are long stretches of sandy beach. Off the beach near my home, big surf driven by a summer south swell often moves massive amounts of sand. When the sand builds bars an excellent (though temporary) break develops which may last hours or several days. Time spent wave watching before paddling out will give clues to the best spots to surf.

Wave Types

Surfers have almost as many ways to describe swells, waves, and surf as Inuits have words for snow. On any beach where surfers gather to watch waves you'll hear about:

Walls are swells that stand up ready to break in lines. Walls peel in shoulders along and off points of land and reefs, and off of peaks at beach breaks.

Peaks occur when walls have a high spot that breaks first. Peaks break in shallower water or because of crossed swells that wedge up into peaks (see *double-ups*).

Tubes pitch out when powerful walls with peaks peel diagonally and form hollow barreling waves. Waves generally tube in water that is relatively shallow in relation to their mass and speed. For example, a five-foot swell reaching land at a sandy beach would start breaking in about seven or eight feet of water. A swell that rushes in from deep water and suddenly impacts with a shallow coral reef will rise suddenly and pitch out to form a tubing wave. This is what happens at the Pipeline on Oahu's North Shore, where some of the best tubing waves in the world are ridden. Powerful swells breaking on prominent reefs or sandbars also create steep and deep waves.

Sections are inconsistent parts of a wave's face that usually fall in front of a surfer and cause a wipeout. Some sectioning waves create tubes if hollow. Riding into a tube from behind is called "shooting a backdoor section."

Bowls occur when a tubing wall turns shoreward due to curving bottom contours. Bowls create a banked track effect on which to make a snap turn off the wave face. Ala Moana Harbor mouth on South

Tubing waves form where powerful swells feel the drag of a quickly shallowing reef. As the wave pitches forward and downward a momentary tunnel is formed. Riding inside a tunnel is every surfers dream.

Here at Waimea Bay, Oahu, the face of this walling wave supports five surfers. In a moment it will steepen, crest, and begin to break across the face.

This wave is closing out and taking two surfers for a wipeout. Note the surfer in the center pearling.

Shore Oahu is a prime example of a bowling reef break (built by the Army Corps of Engineers, by the way).

Double-ups occur when two waves intersect and the combined energy of both throws the lip of the wave out sooner and thicker than the rest of the wave's well. Double-ups near shore produce dangerous up-rush for kids and nonswimmers.

Closeout waves break straight across all at once and dump. Avoid being caught in a closeout. Some surfers enjoy the seconds' brief rush of a closeout ride followed by a crunching wipeout. If you're riding and the wave closes out, time your escape dive as the lip meets the wave trough. Then try to dive through the wave and come out the backside. That's what they do at the Pipeline.

Boils are spots of uprushing water that surface from shallow spots or crevices in the bottom. When the surf is big, boils mark masses of turbulent, unstable water. Boils will often indicate where waves will peak up and break. However, if you sit on the boil it will be almost impossible to catch the wave. Park your board to the side of the upwelling and stay out of the turbulence.

Tides and Surfing

The phenomenon of the rise and fall of the tides along the ocean coasts of the world results from the gravitational pull of the moon and sun.

A set of big swells breaking outside will soon sweep over the gaggle of surfers caught inside.

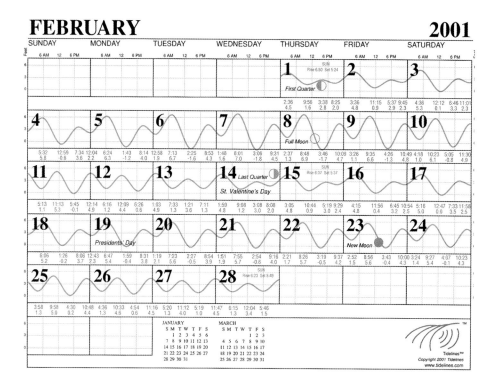

Note the extreme tidal variations between the 9th and 11th of the month. Knowing the tides will help determine if the surf may or may not be good at a particular location. Courtesy: Tidelines

Generally speaking, high tide is the maximum height reached by each rising cycle, and low tide is the minimum water level reached by a falling tide. Technically the term tide refers only to the vertical movement of the water. Horizontal movement of water is actually a tidal current. For example, the extremely swift flow of water in and out of the narrow fjords of Norway, or in and out of coral reefs, is caused by tidal current. The tide period is the interval from low tide to the next recurrent low tide. Tidal periods vary in different parts of the world, but twelve hours and twenty-five minutes is the average interval. Tides are said to advance each day, and the tidal advance also varies. By consulting a tide chart covering my local area, I learn for example, that at Leo Carrillo Beach north of Malibu it's very high tide (+ 0.6) at 10:06 A.M. and quite low (−0.1) at 4:55 P.M. You'll find tidal information for any area you wish to search from a number of sources, such as a coastal newspaper, the aforementioned tide chart, or local lifeguard services. Plan ahead; this is useful information (see Resources).

Here's an example of how tides affect the Leo Carrillo Beach surf-break. On the 27th of October the tide at "Leo" will be high at 9:38

A perfect Pipeline wave and John Peck finds grandeur in the surf. Photo: Judy Rohlof from the Peter Dixon Collection

A.M. and low at 4:16 P.M. So, what do these tidal variations and advances mean to surfers? If you like to surf Leo Carrillo, but don't like fighting in and out over rocks, you'll pick a time of medium to high tide. If you know this point break beach, you'll want to surf it at medium to high tide when the waves have a better shape for surfing and the rocks present less of a hazard.

Knowledge of the local surfing area, plus knowledge of tides and basic oceanography all combine to allow you to make an educated prediction of how the waves will be breaking. Then add information about swell size and direction available from Internet surf sites and you'll score waves more often than not.

Bigger Waves, Better Rides: Intermediate Skills

Becoming a surfer will open a beautiful new world. Making the transition from floundering around in the white-water to actually taking off on a wave and riding it across a cove or bay is one of the most joyous experiences a person can have. Surfing is about being cool under pressure, about being poised, like a matador toying with a bull. Good surfers strive to make their amazing ability look easy. The really great surfers do it naturally. Watching an experienced surfer is a lesson in style and grace in the face of potential disaster. When you reach that point of mastery in the surf, you'll want to ride bigger and better waves. There will come a moment, and you'll never forget it, when you feel in control on the wave. The simple act of surfing, the purity of riding a wave, will grab you

The exciting, flowing energy of surfing is why surfers get so 'stoked' by the sport.

like nothing else. You'll become addicted to surfing and life will change forever. As is often said, there's no such thing as an ex-surfer. How you handle your newfound pleasure is up to you.

In polite, uptight society, identifying yourself as a surfer might not win a lot of points. Forget that. Being a surfer links you to an honorable, centuries-old tribe of people who dared challenge the sea. They found sport and friendship among the waves, and the same happens today, with a few exceptions.

Today, growing numbers of surfers are taking responsibility for the health of the ocean. Organizations such as the Surfrider Foundation, Groundswell Society, and Heal the Bay were founded by surfers, divers, and water people who realized that Mother Ocean needed help. Surfers around the world have taken up the fight to keep the seas healthy. If planet ocean survives our poisons and pollutants so will our sport, and ourselves. So it's okay to be a surfer. Respect surfing's long heritage, the rules of surfing, and enjoy one of the great experiences life has to offer.

With that, let's paddle out and get involved with the waves.

The Rules of Surfing

Because most waves have only enough face to carry one—and occasionally several—surfers, an informal code of conduct has evolved to bring some order to an often chaotic environment. On a typical big-wave day at Malibu's Surfrider Beach, you might see 100 surfers out. Each and every one wants a ride. When 15 or 16 men and women all paddle for the same wave, it's mass mayhem, and very hazardous for all. There's enough slam-bang action for a television wrestling show.

Malibu's outside point, where the waves are biggest, draws the best surfers. The middle break has its share of wannabe hotshots. And the inside section, closest to the beach, where the novice surfers gather, is called "Kiddie Land." When a big set rolls in, a dozen of the outside point riders take off together. Maybe three or four get the wave. They ride into the middle break, where another dozen surfers scramble for the wave. Surfers collide, boards fly, someone gets skegged by a sharp fin or speared by a dagger-pointed board. Three or four survive the mass wipeouts to surf on. These few ride into Kiddie Land where everyone is paddling for the set wave, clueless about what's happening behind and around them. Of the original outside point riders, one is left. He's had a long, bronzed-god ride so far—until some beginner drops in and takes off in front of him. They collide. Boards smash together, fiberglass shatters. The hot surfer is furious. He curses the kook who spoiled "his" wave. Tempers rise. Fists fly. And, the day is ruined for both of them. If the novice had known and followed the rules of the road, all would have gone well. If the hot surfer had been less aggressive on "his" wave and left some room, they'd both be back out on the water.

If we think of surfing as a privilege and not a right, we might all enjoy the sport to its fullest. Crowded waves seem to bring out the beast in some of us, intimidate the novices, and spoil it for those who know how to share. If we observe the common courtesy of give and take in the surf, we'd all catch more waves—despite the hotshots and kooks—and that's what surfing is all about.

Rule Number One

Thou shalt not take off on a wave (drop in, snake, or cut off) in front of someone who has already caught the wave. Dropping in is likely to cause the standing surfer to collide with the offender and result in a double wipeout. This is especially true in steep, fast-breaking surf, with only enough wave face to support a single rider. Sometimes, when the wave is gentle and its face long and broad, it's possible for more than one

Rule of Surfing Number 1: By dropping in, the surfer on the yellow board could very well ruin the ride for the wave rider in front.

person to surf it. This is a judgment call. If you think the wave will take a second rider and drop in, be prepared to pull out so you won't spoil the first surfer's ride. If you do drop in on someone and cause a wipeout, expect hostility or worse.

Rule Number Two

In the lineup, the surfer closest to the breaking part of the wave has the right of way. This is only fair because usually that person has worked his way up to the takeoff spot where the waves break the best. Of course, there are those aggressive types who won't give anyone else a chance at the peak position. How do you handle those hotheads who insist every wave is theirs? If you're a novice there's little you can do except become good enough to outsurf the aggro wave hogs or hope they get tired and paddle in. If you're a local at a certain surfing spot, organize your friends to deal with the situation. Have the biggest guy clearly explain the rules as the rest of you surround the offending surfer. This group enforcement can be done with good humor, which usually brings cooperation.

Rule of Surfing Number 2: Clearly, the surfer in the wetsuit has the right of way. The others nearby should not have attempted to catch the same wave.

At some crowded beaches it's almost impossible to work your way to the best takeoff spot in the lineup, unless you're a really hot surfer or a respected, long-time local. That's why the novice should probably pass up the more popular breaks and gain experience at less-crowded, "mellow" areas. Wherever you paddle out, acknowledge the other surfers with a nod, a smile, or a simple "Hi," and let it go at that for a time. The locals, when they realize you won't drop in on them, or bore them with your life story, will gradually give the newcomer acceptance. Becoming part of the pack may take an hour or several weeks. Your surfing ability will speed the process, but so will courtesy and good humor.

Some years back my wife and I traded houses for six weeks with a couple who lived near Hanalei Bay, Kauai, Hawaii. We had always wanted to surf that fantastic point break. It was spring and everyone said there wouldn't be any surf. We paddled out anyway, just to be surrounded by the bay's beauty. Luck and Mother Nature provided waves, and for the next six weeks, we surfed every day. The news that the surf was up spread rapidly and the locals arrived to dominate their break. We gave them wave space, respect, and acknowledged their status. After a few days of playing it cool we were accepted as part of the crowd and allowed a place in the lineup. On an especially good day of over-head surf, my wife was hanging back a bit, anxious about the power of that fast-breaking right. The local wave "enforcer" noticed her wariness to take off. When a well-formed easy-to-catch swell approached, "The Enforcer" called to the others, "Back off, that's Mama's wave!"

The whole group made room for her in the lineup and chanted, "Go, Mama! Go!" With that encouragement, she paddled, caught the wave and road it fully a quarter mile across the bay. She thanked them as the artist she is, by painting a watercolor of Hanalei Bay and leaving it where the locals gathered at the seaside park. The next day, we found two woven palm frond hats the locals had left where we usually hung out. After that, and until we left, we were part of the bay crew. Patience and respect have their reward in the surfing world.

Rule Number Three

The surfer on the wave always has the right of way. Paddling out into the break while others are riding in often means a possible collision. When paddling out (see discussion on page 73) never place yourself where

Rule of Surfing Number 3: The surfer holding his board and turning turtle failed to move out of the way, so the rider above him wiped out.

you'll spoil the incoming surfer's ride. This means you should paddle around the break. If that's not possible, then you must paddle into the whitewater so the surfer will pass safely in front of you, and you won't spoil his chance of making the wave. You'll get pounded by the whitewater, but your courtesy will be respected and the favor will hopefully be returned. When in doubt, stop paddling, let the standing rider go by, and then get through the wave. We'll discuss paddling out through incoming surf shortly.

A few more cautions. Avoid surfing where there are swimmers or kids playing in the shallows. Your board could hit someone, and if you're surfing without a leash and you lose your board it may wash into someone. Kids will almost always run to grab a loose board and be hit by it. Most public beaches have rules about where and when you can surf. Lifeguard towers will often fly "black ball" flags to signal no-surfing times. Surfers have been fined and even arrested for ignoring the no-surfing black ball. Surf with a heads-up attitude. Be aware of what's happening around you and on the wave you're riding.

Intermediate Surfing Skills

After a few surfing lessons, whether from a friend or a professional, and after enjoying the initial thrills prompted by simply getting up and riding a wave, the beginner is ready for larger, more challenging surf. You'll need to learn how to paddle out and punch through bigger or already broken waves, perfect your takeoff, come to your feet and turn with ease, pull out before a wipeout, and handle yourself when you fall in a large wave. With these skills you can graduate from small waves to larger, more demanding surf. For a new surfer, let's call any wave over three or four feet high.

The new surfer's goal at this point in the learning curve is to master riding safely with others, handle a critical wipeout, and compete successfully for one's share of the waves. Mastering these intermediate skills will allow the beginner to take off on larger, more powerful waves and enjoy the ultimate surfing experience—a fast, controlled ride just in front of the wave's breaking shoulder. Control is the key, because with control the surfer can perform on a wave and ride it to its full potential.

Paddling Out

If inrushing waves prevent you from reaching the lineup, you won't be able to surf. The best way to avoid having to punch through the white-

Paddling out in choppy whitewater. Note that the nose of the board is slightly raised to prevent digging in.

water is to paddle out between sets or work around the breaking waves. Most point and reef breaks will have some sort of channel or calm area where the surf won't be breaking. Spot those areas and use them to your advantage. That's simple enough, but for some reason a lot of beginning surfers don't take time to observe what the waves are doing. With more enthusiasm than caution they launch their boards into the whitewater, and if the waves have any power at all, they get washed back to shore.

When you do paddle out, consider the distance to the lineup. If the break's not far offshore, say 100 yards or so, you can sprint paddle and forget about getting winded. When the lineup is a long way out, you have to judge how good a paddler you are and pace yourself accordingly. So, how do you determine if you're a good paddler or not?

Paddling is an athletic skill that any surfer can learn. The more you paddle your board, the better shape you'll be in and the better you'll be in tune with its individual balance. I've found that on days of little or no surf it's fun just to go for a paddle; it's great for keeping an edge on my fitness. The hours and hours you spend paddling make you a better, stronger surfer and free you from sore muscles. When you're in good paddling shape you catch more waves, escape closeout sets before they crash, and have a lot more fun surfing. So ask yourself: Do I have the paddling skill and strength to catch waves for a couple of hours and to avoid emergency situations? If there's any doubt in your mind about your paddling ability, keep working out on your board.

Some of the outer breaks off Waikiki are a mile offshore, and it takes a strong and experienced paddler to reach the takeoff spot. The old-timers who surf outside Waikiki, guys in their 70s, paddle out there regularly, resting now and then to enjoy the sun coming up over Diamond Head. They catch a few long rides and then paddle back for breakfast.

It's no fun to be halfway out to the lineup, feeling tired and winded, and then be caught inside by a pounding set of waves. When starting out, paddle smoothly with your head up so you can see what's happening and where the surf's breaking. However, no matter how smart you play it, at some point you'll get caught inside and be forced to punch through breaking waves. Depending on the size of the surf, using one or more of the following techniques will get you beyond the whitewater.

Punching Through

If the whitewater is mild, or a wave just about to break is waist-high or smaller, you can plow right through. A few yards before you and the wave meet, paddle harder and build forward momentum. As the

Just making it over a breaking wave.

board's nose smacks into the wave raise your chest, as in a pushup, so the water passes between your body and the board. If the wave seems about to slap you in the face, lower your head and push through the foam. You'll slow somewhat, but keep paddling and get ready to punch through the next one.

Turning Turtle

As wave size increases you'll have to take more aggressive actions, such as "turning turtle," to make it through the whitewater. When the surf grows higher and wave force is sufficient to stop a board from punching through the break, many surfers try turning turtle. They use the board itself as protection from the impact of white water. Turning turtle means flipping over the board and hanging on while the wave passes overhead. If the wave is large, wrap your arms and legs around the board. As the surfer rolls over on his back he pulls the board down, which causes it to act like a sea anchor and helps keep the board, and you, from being washed shoreward. In crowded waves, having the board overhead also protects you from a possible collision or a fin across the scalp.

Turning turtle helps keep you from being swept back to shore.

The Duck Dive

Shortboard riders have discovered that by imitating ducks and other birds that feed underwater they can more easily punch through a breaking wave. The duck dive simulates what a water bird does as a wave approaches. The bird simply dives under the wave and comes up on its backside. The surfer begins a duck dive a few feet before the wave hits by pushing the nose of the board underwater. If the dive is done correctly, you'll surface on the back or seaward side of the wave and not be swept back to shore. The best duck divers calmly face the wave, take a few hard strokes, and get ready to position themselves for the dive. Position and technique are more critical than brute strength. Here are the basic steps of duck diving:

- As the wave approaches, lean forward and grip the board with both hands about a third of its length from the nose.
- In a pushup position, force the nose down about 30 degrees. Your forward momentum will help drive the board downward and underwater. Don't wait too long. Begin to submerge before the wave hits.

The duck dive underwater position prior to surfacing. Note the surfer's leash wrapped around his ankle.

- While still in the pushup position push downward with one knee. Some surfers also push a foot downward to help sink the board. Now get streamlined so you'll offer less resistance to the whitewater.

- When the wave hits, flatten yourself on the board, then angle the nose up slightly. As the wave rolls on bring the nose up higher by pulling it up and pushing the tail down with your knee or foot. You'll surface on the wave's backside and paddle off for the lineup.

All this happens in one smooth motion. Watch how experienced surfers duck dive, imitate them, and practice the technique again and again until you get it right.

Duck diving can be done on a buoyant longboard, but it takes more force to get the nose underwater. On a big longboard, it's probably better to turn turtle. Some longboarders find it easier to tilt the board to the side so a rail more easily slips underwater. As mentioned, be surf-smart and plan your way out to the break so you don't have to fight the whitewater.

On big-wave days it is often impossible to punch through the whitewater to reach the unbroken swells. When the waves are up and pounding in Hawaii, surfers often spend half an hour observing the surf, plotting a safer, easier way out to the lineup. Wave-watching and planning ahead will often save you from being caught inside the breaking waves when a clean up set powers through and wipes everyone out.

Catching Bigger Waves

You're in the lineup now and it's time to catch some waves. Your goal is to learn how to take off, come to your feet, and control the board well enough to make the wave. Wannabe surfers have no right to endanger others and spoil rides if they haven't learned the basics of board control. Recently, at Maui's famous Honolua Bay, I watched a muscled heavyweight beginner on a 10-foot longboard repeatedly taking off in the middle of the crowd. The guy had no idea of what he was doing. Wave after wave, he'd wipe out and take five or six surfers over the falls with him. Because of his aggressive, out-of-control technique he tired quickly and almost drowned in a closeout set. I think the locals all knew what would eventually happen and decided to let the sea enforce its punishment.

Control is essential. When you have board control you've graduated to the ultimate surfing experience—making a fast-breaking wave and riding a moving mountain of cascading water across a bay, cove, or inlet. Control means being able to turn, cut back into the breaking wave, avoid other surfers, and maneuver with sufficient skill to make the most out of the ride. Surfing is so much fun when it finally comes together and you're one with the board and wave. Here comes a nice smooth swell rising over the reef. Go for it. Take off!

The Takeoff

To successfully take off and catch a wave you must be in the proper place in the lineup—and that's close to where the surf is breaking, or will break. Watch where the more experienced surfers place themselves in the lineup. That's where you want to be. If possible, have an experienced surfer judge the wave for you and do exactly as instructed. It may take time to work up to the takeoff spot, but you won't catch a wave if you don't.

Starting the ride in medium surf (waves three to five feet high) calls for paddling full out. If you can't match your speed as best you can with the wave's speed it will pass under you. Start paddling early enough so the wave won't break on you before going down the face. How early is early? A wave that can be easily caught has not yet crested and has a steep face that looks like it's close to breaking. The angle of slope will be steep, but not yet vertical. The steeper the wave, the more critical the takeoff becomes.

If the top of the wave rising behind you already shows whitewater you're facing a late takeoff and will probably get dumped. When I first paddle out, and I'm not sure where the best takeoff spot is, I keep going seaward until I'm beyond the break. Now in calm water, I can observe what the swells are doing and catch my breath. In a few minutes I'll get sense of where the best takeoff spot is and begin paddling in for the break. I'll also be constantly looking out to sea and scanning the water, looking for a rising unevenness of the normally flat horizon that tells me a set of swells is approaching. The greater the rise, the larger the arriving surf. Sometimes experienced surfers will stand on their boards for a better view of the swells. When really big swells are spotted they'll warn, *"Outside!"* and everyone will begin paddling seaward to escape a closeout set.

A clean, graceful takeoff followed by a turn away from the breaking wave will help determine how well the remainder of the ride goes. If the takeoff is late you'll be in a critical situation with little time to set up for the ride to come. If you paddle too soon, before the wave has enough slope to propel the board down the wave's face, you'll go nowhere.

The slope of the wave also determines when and how you'll paddle and take off. Too little slope; no wave to ride. If the swell is overly steep and close to breaking, you'll suddenly be engulfed in a falling, pounding wave. It won't take long to recognize if the approaching wave is going to close out and crash. If you sense you'll be caught inside the break, swivel the board around and paddle over the top of the wave before it shows whitewater. When you do find a spot near the break and decide to take off, you'll need only a few strokes to start the slide. Start paddling a moment or so before the wave peaks behind you. Take a final look behind and decide if the wave is going to dump on you or if its holding good shape. If it's a go, and the downward slide begins, paddle a few strokes more to keep the nose up. If you feel that the nose might submerge, arch your back, which shifts the center of balance a bit to the rear. This brings the nose up and you've caught the wave.

If the wave is steep you'll want to angle sharply away from the breaking portion so the nose of the board won't dig in and send you flying off. On a gentle wave with a moderate slope the takeoff angle is only a few degrees off straight ahead. At surf spots like Waikiki and San Onofre, California, where waves are shallow faced, they can be caught by paddling almost straight off.

Standing (Dropping In)

Coming to your feet while sliding down a wet, moving wave that's about to break then turning to set up for the ride requires that several movements occur simultaneously. It may seem difficult, but our remarkable bodies can pull it all together if we don't let fear dominate our will. Catching a wave, standing, and putting the board in best trim for the ride all comes naturally when we have a go-for-it attitude. However, a few fundamentals will prove helpful.

Wait two or three seconds before standing. Let the feeling of the slide tell you that you've caught the wave. There's no mistaking that first moment of downward acceleration. Beginners often jump to their feet the moment they sense the board moving on its own. It takes a couple of seconds or so for the board to pick up speed and stabilize. Trust your instincts. You'll "feel" that special moment of the slide beginning and know it's time to stand.

When changing from a paddling to a standing position grab the rails below your chest and push up hard. At the same time, in a single smooth, continuous movement, pop up to a crouched position with one leg forward. Ideally, you'll be in a low "power crouch" rather than standing straight up like a totem pole. Think of how a boxer stands ready to advance or retreat, but always in balance. Your chest should be facing forward with your shoulders at right angles to the centerline of the board. Set your feet fairly wide apart, centered on the deck at a right angle to the length of the board. This will put you in a secure, stable position. Bend your knees slightly, extend your arms for balance, and face the direction you're going. Think of your arms as wings of a bird as you fly across the wave. Hit this position correctly and your previously tippy board suddenly becomes stable and away you go. Keep looking ahead and maintain that power crouch. With a little practice, coming to your feet and taking a balanced stance seems quite natural.

A mini-hint: Focus your eyes up and ahead, not on the board's nose. This seems to detach your attention for the ride to come instead of the possibility of wiping out on takeoff. And one more: Long toenails sometimes drag or catch on the board's deck.

Turning

Turning movements can be powerful and abrupt, or slight and fluid. The wave, and where you are on it, determines how forceful your turn must be. Turning in easy-breaking rolling surf, where the wave face is shallow and smooth, calls for smooth, fluid movements. As waves grow steeper and faster, you'll need more powerful and abrupt turns to keep ahead of the breaking shoulder. After a few rides, turning by leaning and shifting your weight will flow effortlessly together, and you, the board, and the wave will be in harmony.

As the slide down the wave face begins and you stand, it's time to turn away from the breaking shoulder. A board turns because of the drag or friction being applied to one side or the other. Since the fin (or fins) keeps the board on a straight course and helps prevent it from sideslipping down a wave, its resistance to turning must be overcome. To counter the fin's function, the surfer's rear foot creates resistance by pushing down on the stern of the board. The more downward push, the more friction, and the faster the board will turn. A really hard downward push will produce a radical turn that leads to stalling or kicking out of the wave. After a little practice the amount of force needed to turn the board become intuitive.

You can make slight turns and corrections to your board's trim by leaning to one side or the other and moving forward and back. *Slight* means just a few degrees off the board's center. The more you lean and force the tail down, the greater and faster the turn. As you lean, water is pressurized under the board and it wants to get out. The more downward force you create, the more you'll accelerate (like a high pressure hose pushes back the nozzle). Shifting your weight forward, which puts the board's nose down, will increase speed. Moving back will dig in the board's tail, slowing it. All the while, your eyes will be telling you where to aim the nose of the board. If another surfer is sitting inside, you'll either have to turn around him to avoid a collision or kick out of the wave.

You can use the basic turns discussed here in various combinations. It is very important to practice surfing to the left and right. It's all too easy to be come habituated to surfing in one direction. It's my guess that half the world's waves break to the right and the other half to the left. You'll catch more waves if you can ride them in either direction.

The Bottom Turn

Add the bottom turn to your growing repertoire and you can control the board in most situations. The bottom turn is useful because it allows the board and rider to gain a lot of speed as they slide for the bottom of the wave, which is important in big surf, where the rider needs great speed to outrace the huge wall of water rising above him and reach the unbroken wave face. Without sufficient speed to escape the breaking wave, the surfer will be caught under a collapsing mountain of water.

Pahl Dixon cranking a bottom turn on a fast breaking Malibu wave. Dixon photo

The bottom turn is a powerful, fluid, high-speed maneuver. As the turn begins, the body rotates slightly ahead of the foot action, making it appear that the surfer is off balance. Actually the rider is directly in line with the center of the board, somewhat like a motorcycle racer going into a sweeping, high-speed turn. Even in moderate size surf, a bottom turn will help give you extra speed to accelerate or begin other maneuvers such as a cutback or kickout. When it all comes together, a coordinated bottom turn will send you up the face of the wave for the next maneuver.

To perform a bottom turn you must delay cutting away from the break and drop rapidly down the wave's face, which greatly increases speed. When the board reaches the almost-flat portion of the wave-front, you'll make an aggressive turn, leaning into the wave, and away from the breaking whitewater. Before the board slows and begins to stall you then use its momentum to climb the face of the unbroken wave and trim across the wall, pull an off-the-lip maneuver, or kick out. A strong, well-executed bottom turn is a must for anyone serious about surfing.

During the drop, keep your weight back to prevent the board's nose from digging in and pearling. This position also keeps the fin in the wave and prevents sideslipping. Drive the tail and fin in deep, using pressure from your rear foot and hips during the turn. This forceful motion buries the rail and accelerates the turn.

Many big wave–surfers let their hands point the way to the turn's pivot point, the spot where the surfer will make the turn. Pointing to where you'll turn helps position the body in the direction it needs to go.

In Hawaii, at Sunset Beach for example, the faces of these giant waves are steep and rough when the offshore winds are blowing. Often surfers are blown back, airborne, over the crests of these huge breakers. The tumbling, out-of-control fall into the trough can be a surfer's worst nightmare. In these conditions, big wave–riders find it mandatory to take off and drop for the bottom before turning.

The Top Turn

The top turn is for less-steep waves that require immediate trim to catch. Rather than dropping to the trough of the wave before turning, you turn immediately up near the crest and start angling for speed. This is a good way to set up for a noseride. A face turn is just that— you turn when you've dropped halfway or less down the wave, a must when taking off on a wave that's about to tube. If the board feels like it's slipping, then weight the tail to keep the fin(s) in the water so as to avoid spinning out.

David McCauley turns off the lip of the wave at Margaret River main break, Western Australia. Photo Courtesy Garth Sports Pty. Ltd.

Kicking Out

When you learn to kick out aggressively, escaping a collision with another surfer or escaping a wave that's closing out in front of or around you is no big deal. Because it's sometimes necessary to kick out in a microsecond to escape a wipeout, it has to be done forcefully. Start the turn by shoving the tail down with your rear foot to sink the back of the board. This stalls the board and starts it turning up the face of the wave. At the same time rotate your body in the direction of the turn, which helps the board swing. If the turn and body rotation all come together with sufficient force, the surfer will go over the top of the wave and pull out of the break.

Trim

After catching the wave, standing, and turning from the break the surfer must stabilize the board for the ride to come. This is called *trimming*, and it helps you control the board in all size waves with minimal friction and maximum thrust. When a board is in trim for the wave you're

With good balance the surfer has her board in trim.

riding you'll go faster, be in balance, and wipe out less. On fast-breaking waves, trimming for speed can mean the difference between having the wave close out around you and safely outracing the break. Trim too low and you slow down, trim too high and you'll slide out of the wave or stall. Each board comes into trim differently, just as each wave is different. Shortboards tend to be less stable and require more attention to bring into trim. In slow, lazy waves the best trim will have you riding almost straight off. On steep, near closeout waves you trim for maximum speed by dropping the nose and moving the weight forward.

Walking the Board

To change a longboard's balance point to drop its nose and accelerate, it's necessary to move forward by "walking" the board, since leaning forward or back on a longboard won't greatly alter the center of balance. Quickly moving backward or forward will, though. On-the-nose surfing is possible only when the rider can move forward, then return to a stable position. Some surfers shuffle to the nose, others actually walk, placing one foot in front of another. This can be practiced with the board on the sand. Once you feel comfortable stepping forward and back it's time to try hot-dogging. This old style of longboard nose riding allows maneuvers such as hanging five or ten toes over the nose of the board.

Noseriding contests were big events in the 1960s. Special boards were built with weighted sterns and winged fins that would allow long rides with the surfer perched on the very tip of the surfboard. This up forward surfing style gives a great feeling of speed. When it all comes together the sensation is almost as if there were no board under you. To hang five or ten toes over the nose the board needs to be in perfect trim, with the tail held down by the breaking wave. At one famous hang ten contest Micky Munoz walked to the nose, planted himself there, and proceeded to ride a third of a mile hanging ten. He won the contest and his far forward nose ride has yet to be beaten. So for fun, for showing off a bit, and to demonstrate your growing ability, try riding the nose.

When you have the ability to take off, turn, trim, cut back, and kick out it's time to dare riding closer to the curling portion of the waves. That's when surfing gets truly exciting. From there it's not far to learn the art of tube riding. As surf expert/editor Sam George wrote, "To walk the nose is to dance. Hitting the lip [of the wave] is athletic. Riding the tube is where surfing becomes an art."

Sideslipping

Sometimes you'll want to break your fin(s) free from the wave to slow down for a tube ride or do advanced tricks such as drifting turns and 360s. This requires sideslipping. To begin to slip, you need to feel the flow of the water under the board at the particular moment of turning. The basic movement is somewhat like sliding an offroad bike or automobile through a dirt road turn. It's almost the same as a surfboard. While trimming across the wave, shift your weight forward to dig the front edge of the board into the face of the wave, thereby reducing the relative grip of the back rail. This causes the back of the board and fin to lose grip in the wave and it will begin to sideslip. To stop a sideslip, move your weight back and dig in the tail rail. This is the same sort of edge control that skiers and snowboarders use. Some surfers drag a hand in the wave, which also causes the board to rotate and helps keep one's balance. Controlled sideslips and spins demand lots of practice and are usually learned from trial and error. Keep watching the experts sideslip and you'll subconsciously pick up on their technique.

Accidental sideslips often occur over boils and on steep waves, leading to unexpected wipeouts. Once you get used to sideslipping it's easy correct a potential spinout by planting your back foot to sink the rail and fin(s) into blue water again.

Tube Riding

Trimming the board through a barreling wave is much the same, except that an even finer line is required to make your body fit inside the tube. Taking a wide power stance and lowering yourself to a squatting position helps in a smallish barrel. Most times its possible to surf through the initial collapse of the wave by going for maximum speed. Sometimes the wave will suddenly collapse behind you, compressing the air inside the tube. The resulting rush of escaping air often blows the rider out of the tube, saving him from being caught inside a barrel wipeout. Surfers who love tube riding say that when the wave gets critical, hang in the tube as long as possible. When you're knocked off the board, jump away from it and swim out the back of the wave. I know it's easier to write about this than race out of a collapsing tube. And, I'll gladly admit that I'm not a Pipeline veteran. However, I've been inside those green cylindrical walls a few times and the wet-and-wild ride is well worth the usual crunching wipeout.

Tube riding requires very symmetrical and steep waves that break over reefs to form barrels wide enough to ride through. That's why there are really very few places where these rolling tubes form consis-

In the tube, the ultimate fun experience.

tently. For decades surfers have been drawn to Oahu's North Shore to challenge the Pipeline and other tube riding spots.

Wipeouts

Wiping out is inevitable, so you might as well be prepared. Here are some suggestions to ease the pain and get you back to shore safely.

Protect yourself by avoiding impact with your board and the bottom by doing whatever it takes. You are mostly water, and of course a swimmer, or you wouldn't be out there. Swim around in the wave after you wipe out to position yourself against impact with board or bottom. The better position is feet down with your hands and fingers interlocked over your head to soften a potential blow. If that's not possible, curl up like a sleeping baby and be ready to fight your way to the surface when the battering subsides.

In a bad wipeout, trust your instincts. Your body will know what to do if you don't allow panic to take over. Survival instincts make experienced surfers automatically wriggle like a fish in emergency situations to avoid going over the falls and/or hitting the bottom. This ability to

Sky surfers. Dixon photo

escape catastrophes comes naturally if you keep your eyes open, cheeks puffed out to hold that extra bit of air, and a smile. Really, forcing a smile helps control panic. When you get totally thrashed and feel like you were mugged by five sumo wrestlers, there's always prayer. Then there's letting go and relaxing to conserve your breath. That's my favorite when the want of air becomes critical.

If your dream is to someday challenge heavy waves, count on being wiped out again and again. When the inevitable big wave wipeout comes, keep the faith and know you'll survive. Some big wave–surfers, when things get critical, shift their perspective from personal fear to watching themselves from afar. If you can see yourself and think, "Wow, that person is really taking it down there." Then you can feel detached, even see the humor of it, which conserves energy by relieving anxiety. A few basics for surviving wipeouts:

- Be in good physical condition and swim well.
- Have a buddy watching out for you, just in case you float to the surface and need help.
- Protect your head from board and bottom impact.
- If surfing bigger waves isn't fun, don't do it.
- Always stay focused on the moment, take charge of the situation, and you'll survive hundreds of wipeouts.

As your surfing skills improve, you may become one of those surf travelers who climb aboard the big bird for the winter migration to the North Shore, Bali, Fiji or wherever the waves break hard and clean. Have fun, good surf, and good luck.

Safety

Surfing continues to lure increasing numbers of people into the waves. Most new surfers are pulled in by the challenge, the sport's simple beauty, and the urge to share it all with likeminded adventurous friends. For a few it's a macho thing, a bravado show-off compulsion, devoid of appreciation for the naturalness of the sea and the spiritual uplift that surfing brings. We who sit in the lineup watching the horizon hoping for a great wave also see small baitfish swimming under our boards, the blend of shore and sea, and the graceful flight of pelicans coasting effortlessly along the face of a swell. Perhaps we'll also ponder our mortality, or nature. Surfing brings us these sights and reflections. After a horrifying wipeout, when death was perhaps seconds away, one thinks about life and how dangerous Mother Ocean can be. If you haven't done so already, you decide it's time to start working out, time to become a skilled, strong swimmer, and time to become a real waterman or waterwoman.

One can't control the ocean, and those who spend real time on or in it wouldn't want to try.

Checking the break for hazards is always a good idea before paddling out.

Watermen and waterwomen know intrinsically how to coexist with the sea. Not to conquer or to best it, but to be part of it. The more a surfer knows about the ocean and how to handle oneself in it, the safer surfing becomes. Become a waterman or waterwoman, for doing so will lift your self-esteem, give you acceptance in the lineup, heighten the joy you receive from the ocean, and may even save your life.

Any accident, even a single act of poor judgment, can lead to drowning, which claims thousands of lives each year—deaths that could have been prevented had the victim been waterwise. Poor swimmers, ignorant boaters, untrained skin- and scuba-divers, reckless Jet-Skiers, and surfers who paddle into waves beyond their ability may add to the alarming death by drowning statistics. Though surfing is statistically safer that most action sports, deaths and serious accidents do occur. Safety by, on, and under the water boils down to these seven basics:

1. *Know your limitations.* If you can't swim and paddle well, stay out of big surf until you've learned these skills. If you chill quickly, even in warm water, wear a wetsuit.

2. *Understand the dangers of surfing.* You'll be safer when you can spot ripcurrents, where waves close out, and underwater hazards such as reefs and rocks before paddling out.

3. *Learn the hazards* before *paddling out.* Always ask local surfers and lifeguards about hazards. Many hazards can be spotted from the beach, so take time to look.

4. *Become a strong, oceanwise swimmer.* Train for and practice swimming in the ocean. You should be able to swim a half mile without tiring.

5. *Master and practice rescue skills.* Take an American Red Cross lifesaving class, first aid class, or both. CPR is a must. Many surfers traveling afar become basic Emergency Medical Technicians.

6. *Anticipate dangers before they happen.* Think ahead, spot rips, floating logs, and other hazards. Observe the time between sets of waves so you won't be caught in dangerous closeout surf.

7. *Stay alert to changing conditions.* The direction and size of swells may change rapidly. Gentle waves may suddenly become big and gnarly. Approaching storms could bring lightning. If in doubt, paddle in.

Drownings don't just happen. They're preventable. A drowning, or a bad surfing accident, is a culmination of a chain of events that began when someone screwed up, was careless, or knowingly took an unreasonable chance with his or someone else's life. It's usually the novice surfer who gets in trouble because of lack of training, skill, and experience. And often, a foolhardy surfer or beginner endangers someone else's life.

Colliding with another surfer, or being hit by your own board, is the number one cause of surfing accidents.

Being safe in the water is so simple. Think and plan ahead: A few minutes watching the waves, observing currents, and detecting hazards makes surfing safer. Avoid situations where collisions are likely, where waves can't be ridden safely, and where rocks and ripcurrents create hazards. All can be avoided if you know what to look for. If I had $10 for every wide-eyed novice surfer or swimmer that Oahu North Shore lifeguards pulled from a ripcurrent or pounding shorebreak in the last two decades, I'd have a new BMW in my garage.

How does 70-year-old Peter Cole, North Shore pioneer big wave–surfer, continue to ride the heavies at Sunset and Waimea? He's a waterman! He knows his surf turf and personal limitations. Cole doesn't take off until he's sure he can make the wave. Sure, he catches fewer waves, but he's out there with the kids doing his big-wave thing. When Peter paddles into the lineup at Sunset the crew cheers his arrival. He survives and endures because he is a marvelous, wave-wise swimmer, knows the break, and is in fantastic condition for a man his age.

The surfers who endure, who keep surfing into the sunset, have that go-for-it character backed up by experience and skill in the sea. Without it, you'll never have the respect of the real surfers and the honored title of "waterman" or "waterwoman."

Remember the first rule of surfing from chapter 4? On a fast-breaking wave with little room for another rider, it's bad judgment and

Young Karina Petroni's soft nose guard protects herself and others from being speared. Photo: Erik Petroni, courtesy SurfCo Hawaii

downright selfish to drop in ahead of the surfer who has the wave. That's inviting a collision as well as spoiling the wave for the person who caught it first.

Most surfing accidents are caused by collisions with other boards or rocks, or by a blasting wipeout in the shorebreak. Many accidents occur when a beginner's board pearls, shoots up in the air, and comes down hard on its owner or another person. This won't happen if the surfer knows how to control his board. No one has any business surfing in crowded waves if they can't control the direction of their board. In emergencies a skilled surfer can cut back and turn, stall, and make a successful pullout to avoid a collision. *A novice must learn these basic maneuvers before joining the crowd in the line up.* Too many beginners take off on a wave with little or no ability to control their board.

Wipeouts

Wipeouts are as much a part of surfing as the waves themselves, and the subject of endless talk. Wipeouts occur frequently, and their severity depends on several factors. In deep water with no rocks or reef below the surface, they're not as dangerous as a ride "over the falls" in

Late takeoffs usually result in wipeouts.

the shorebreak. It's the hard wipeout in a tangle of surfers and flying boards that sometimes ends up with someone missing teeth or a winning a row of sutures in his or her scalp.

How to avoid wipeouts? Simple: kick out of the wave before it becomes critical. Probably a half of all wipeouts result from staying in the wave too long. It's natural to want to ride to the wave's limit, but that's like playing against a Las Vegas dealer—you're bound to lose most of the time. Don't take off on a wave that's about to break more quickly than you can react. Going over the falls and into a cement mixer of wild water can take the fun out of surfing. Really; it's not necessary to catch every wave that lifts the tail of your board. If you're one of those "My wave!" surfers, slow down a little, take a look around and savor the moment. You'll catch your breath and do better on the next wave.

It's easy to recognize a wipeout before it happens. The wave you're paddling to catch suddenly steepens and crests, and it's probably already too late for a takeoff. Then the wave pitches forward and a blast of whitewater begins to tower over and around you. A microsecond later you pearl, go over the falls, and wipe out. Better wave judgment would have prevented that. If the wave wasn't critically steep the wipeout could be controlled by riding in on the whitewater lying prone, remembering to shift your weight back to keep the board's nose from digging in.

Experienced surfers often ride the soup to shore standing. This is a skill that needs to be practiced if you're going to surf safely. It's certainly okay for a beginner to head in lying on the board. Riding prone gives you more control of the board so it won't strike you or someone else. If you're on the board you'll avoid a walk in over rocks.

If the wipeout is violent and you lose the board, try to keep it away from you by diving deep or rolling away. Because of the leash, you'll have a sense of where it may be. A board that dives deeply is going to come up again with a lot of force. Protect yourself by folding your arms around your head—and stay underwater until the white water has passed by, which you'll feel. Also, if at all possible, try to avoid falling on the shore side of the board. This eliminates one possibility of the board smashing into you. In shorebreak surf where it's shallow, this is particularly important.

Big-Surf Wipeouts

Big-surf wipeouts present a double danger. Beginners, and those without a lot of big-wave experience, shouldn't place themselves and others in danger by taking waves beyond their ability. That's common sense. But some surfers want to make a name for themselves and push it beyond their personal limits in a quest for glory. Not smart.

For a novice, big surf might mean five-foot waves. (For the North Shore crew a big wave wipeout is 20 feet plus.) Whatever the size of the wave, wipeout dangers are much the same. The first is being hit by the board. The second is the tremendous pounding you'll take as tons of water smash you downward.

Big wave–surfers tell of being driven deep underwater by giant waves and losing all sense of direction. They'll swear they were held down a minute or longer and came close to passing out. Except in the biggest surf, that's likely an exaggeration, but 15 to 30 seconds is not unusual. That's a long time underwater when you're being pummeled, your wind's gone, and panic is seconds away. This will be followed by the danger of another closeout set rolling in on top of you.

If there's ever a time to control panic and remain calm it's now. Relax. Don't struggle and use up what oxygen is left in your lungs. Within seconds the wave will pass. You'll feel a momentary calm. Head for daylight, and if you've become disoriented, look for the light. If you can, push off the bottom for the surface, and when you reach air and gulp in a lungful; there's a good chance another wave will be steamrolling down and the whitewater is so thick you'll suck in foam. At this point, if you're thinking at all, you'll ask, "What am I doing out here?" Don't panic. Even in smaller waves a bad wipeout can push the body to the edge of unconsciousness. If you're tired, scared, and in waves beyond your surfing and swimming ability, bad things can happen in a hurry. I still can't forget one wipeout I had at a California winter surf spot. After an hour of riding demanding five-foot waves, and after a few average wipeouts, I was beginning to feel cold and tired. An inner survival instinct warned me it was time to catch a wave in, but the conscious ego-driven side of my brain said, "Just one more big one."

A few minutes later the horizon was filled with a line of huge swells that were unlike anything that had rolled through all morning. Someone yelled, "Outside," and we all began paddling to position ourselves for a takeoff. I let the other surfers have a wave and paddled for what I thought was the last one in the set. As I slid down the face and stood the wave pitched out above me. There was no time to kick out and I bailed. I was pounded, driven into the rocky bottom, and pummeled badly. Painfully, my shoulder hit a boulder. Then my ankle was tugged viciously and I realized my leash had become entangled in rocks on the bottom. As I had practiced on the beach, I reached for the

Most wipeouts can be avoided with a heads up, aware attitude. If not, be in good enough physical condition to survive them.

ankle strap and tried to free the Velcro closure, but before I could unfasten it another wave blasted me.

Panic was close at hand, but I forced myself to relax. By that point my lungs screamed for air and I began seeing little bright starbursts. Then my fingers found the tab that would release the strap. I freed it and shot for the surface. The set had passed and I gulped enough air to keep me conscious. Next, I had to free my board from its leash. I untied the leash from the board but couldn't free the cord from its hold in the rocks. At that point another set of heavies rolled in and ripped the board out of my exhausted arms. Now I was really tired and faced a long swim to the beach against a current that was taking me into the rocks. My experience as a competitive swimmer, and beach lifeguard—my work to become a waterman—all combined to help me and I made shore safely. Thinking about it later, I realized that I should have listened to that inner warning to paddle in while it was safe to do so. After all, there will be another day, another wave.

Besides being a real waterman, and in superb physical condition, a big wave–surfer must have the confidence needed to take off on those awesome giants.

Brock Little, one of the North Shore greats, believes confidence born from experience is the key to surfing big waves. Ken Bradshaw, who helped pioneer giant-wave tow-in surfing, has ridden some of the largest waves ever. His training is focused not so much on surfing as surviving a long, punishing wipeout. Bradshaw prepares for big Hawaiian surf wipeouts by skin-diving into the lava caves found amid offshore reefs. Repetitive, prolonged dives built his confidence and ability to stay under when the big one occurs.

The Bailout

Unlike defensive maneuvers such as turning turtle, duck diving, or punching through, which we discussed in detail in chapter 4, the bailout is the surfer's last resort for staying safe—perhaps for surviving.

Imagine that you're paddling out when a big wave begins to close out in front of you. You realize quickly that there's no chance to make it over the crest or paddle sideways and climb over the wave's shoulder. In the next couple of seconds you decide that none of the defensive maneuvers you know will help in this instance. If that wave looks so awesome that you're certain you can't get through it, bail out early and make your dive to escape the wave's force. As I've mentioned before, try to keep control of your board; if you lose it, it can hurt you or someone else. Before abandoning ship make sure there's nobody

A last-resort bailout. With any luck he'll escape being hit by the board.

behind you. If there is, hang on to the board at all costs. When you bail, push the board *to the side* and away from you. This will help reduce the chance of being hit when you, the board, and all that falling water mix it up. Next, attempt to dive under and through the wave. If that doesn't work, relax and let the power of the wave subside and then retrieve the board. If you can't release it from the grip of the white water, then flow in with the broken wave. Back to basics.

Ripcurrents and Wild Water

Ripcurrents and rough seas cause most emergencies at the beach. On a hard-driving big surf day along crowded beaches in Hawaii or Southern California, rip rescues may total several hundred. Off Zuma Beach, California, a giant fast-moving rip once sucked 28 swimmers 150 yards offshore. Conditions were so hazardous in the pounding surfline that the guards couldn't bring the victims in, and both victims and rescuers were pulled to safety by lifeguard boats and deposited several miles away at the nearest pier. Sunset Beach, Hawaii, is perhaps the king of rip-makers. In the early 1960s, seven servicemen were caught in an extremely strong rip and swept rapidly seaward. Before help came, they all drowned. Another classic rip rescue occurred when an inexperienced surfer was caught in the Sunset rip and swept far out, where he couldn't make it back on his own. A rescue helicopter landed on the beach, picked up all-time waterman Buzzy Trent and his board, and flew him out to the exhausted surfer. Buzzy and board dropped into the water and he guided the unfortunate surfer back safely to the beach.

Right now let's dispel the notion that ripcurrents are "undertows" or "tide." There's no such thing as an undertow, and while tides in certain situations can increase the chance of rips, they shouldn't be confused with them. Like waves, no two beaches are the same. The best way to avoid a fast ride seaward in a flowing rip is to spot it from the beach. Should you get caught in a rip, being able to recognize where it's going will allow you to safely swim from its grasp.

Most rips are caused by massive amounts of seawater piling up in the shallows near shore. This water must find a way to flow back seaward and seek its natural level. Water will always take the path of least resistance, and often this outflowing current will scour out a channel,

Where waves are big and the bottom uneven, ripcurrents will almost always be present. Dixon photo

which increases the seaward flow, and a strong ripcurrent develops. A rip can also occur when two opposing currents meet and when water builds against headlands and must find a way to flow outward. Sometimes rips flow along shore where the currents have dug a trench. Rips move seaward quite quickly, racing out a quarter of a mile and more at speeds of four to five miles an hour.

Rips can usually be seen from the beach, if you know what to look for. As the outward flow of water speeds up and digs a trough, it picks up sand and holds it in suspension. The suspended sand gives the water a slightly off-color appearance. If there's silt present, the look will be muddy with off-color foam along the rip's boundary. I recall standing on the bluff overlooking Zuma Beach and seeing at least 15 super rips along a mile-long stretch of shore. At some beaches, rips can occur every 20 yards, giving the shore a scalloped appearance. Called gutter rips, these shallow-water rips are particularly dangerous because they can quickly sweep little kids off their feet and into over-the-head water. On a big-surf day at Venice Beach, California, two lifeguards and I made 54 gutter-rip rescues. We were wet from mid-morning until the crowd left in late afternoon.

Most rips are not very wide, perhaps 20 to 30 yards at the most. Even a strong swimmer will have trouble overcoming a fast-moving

The Coast Guard picked up this surfer after a rip current has swept him almost a mile from shore.

rip. The general rule is not to fight the current, but to float with it until the rip diminishes, get out of the current, then swim in where it isn't. Sometimes you can escape a rip by swimming diagonally across the current. The best course for a surfer or swimmer is to avoid a rip. Learn to recognize rip conditions. At an unfamiliar beach ask the locals or a lifeguard about rips or other hazards.

Judging Waves

Judging where, when, and how waves will break is an important part of surfing and being safe in the surf. Knowing with a fair degree of certainty how a wave will form, crest, and break allows the surfer to make a educated decision to take off or not. The better you can judge a wave, the more confidence and success you'll have catching one.

Here's a typical scenario: You're on the beach watching swells wrap around a headland, feel the drag of the bottom, and become surf. The waves have little shape today and are breaking top to bottom with no clearly defined shoulder. Since you've watched this break several times, you know it's not happening. The wind is from the wrong direction and a low tide has exposed the rocky flats just offshore. After another half hour of wave watching, you witness two overhead closeout sets that sweep across the entire surfing area. You think about what would have happened if you'd been paddling out when they arrived so unexpectedly.

Two weeks later you return to the same beach and are greeted by fantastic overhead surf. A warm sun glitters on the blue water and the wind has yet to ruffle the calm surface. The swells wrapping around the point are in the right direction, the tide's high, and every wave has a ridable shoulder. Even better, you've got the whole break to yourself. Cowabunga! Let's go surfing!

You grab your board and start for the water. Before paddling out you take a final look seaward. Be aware of another cardinal rule of surfing: Expect anything, perhaps the most beautiful set of waves to ever come around the headland, or on the other extreme, jellyfish, a sheen of oil on the water, a shark's dorsal fin, some green sea snakes, or whatever. Be alert to that ever-changing, potentially dangerous, and always exciting ocean you're paddling out to.

Marine Life Hazards

Did someone mention sharks?

Of the 250 or so species of sharks only a few are considered dangerous. But they're out there swimming just below the surface—big, mean, and hungry in all the seas of the world. If you surf, accept that they're there. If you can't, stay out of the water. Shark attacks occur in the tropics and cold seas, in shallows and in deep water. Most verified shark attacks have occurred off Australia's eastern beaches—over 250 fatalities in the past 100 years. Australians and South Africans have gone to great effort to protect their swimmers, using shark patrols, netting, watchtowers and aerial patrols to safeguard bathers. Every year about a dozen attacks are reported, and each incident draws media attention. How many photos have you seen of a surfer holding his board and pointing to a half-oval gap in the foam caused by a shark's bite? While the attention-getting photos lead to calls for "something to be done," most incidents are quickly forgotten, except by surfers and skin-divers, who live with the possibility of a shark encounter every time they enter the water.

The chance of meeting an aggressive shark is very remote. Along the California coast there are an average of two non-fatal incidents a year, and one fatality about every five years. You're safer in the water than driving to the beach. Large sharks are predators, like seagoing lions or wolves. Their eating habits are indiscriminate. Sharks will feed on anything with food value. They'll "taste" any object, such as a surf-

Are those wiggling toes shark bait?

board, and usually reject it. Here are some basics that shark experts agree on:

- Sharks depend as much on their sense of smell as their sight for locating food. Blood in the water and the vibration of wounded prey attract sharks far beyond their range of vision.
- Sharks are attracted by both living and dead food. Surfing near a rookery of seals or sea lions, or where fishermen are chumming, is not smart.
- Sharks can attack from any angle. They do not have to roll over to bite.
- There is no single tactic used by sharks when attacking. Some attacks are leisurely and deliberate, others are lightning fast without warning.
- A 100-percent effective shark repellent has yet to be developed.

The safest action to take after sighting a shark is to leave the area quickly with as little panic as possible. Thrashing the water will only betray your location and excite the shark. Paddle smoothly and quietly toward shallow water. If the shark makes an aggressive pass, and it appears an attack is imminent, use your surfboard as a shield. Many surfers have used this last-ditch defense successfully, so it's worth a try. Although sharks normally avoid the shallows, don't count on this. While skin-diving off Malibu I was buzzed by a six-foot shark that followed me into three-foot-deep water, at which point I panicked and sprinted for the beach.

Things That Sting

Sea Urchins. Spiny sea urchins are frequently found in great numbers in tropical waters and off the beaches of Southern California. The urchin (called *vana* in Hawaii) looks like a large purple pincushion with long sharp needles protruding from its oval shell. These spines discourage most marine creatures from feasting on them, though urchin divers and sea otters have no problem harvesting them. The surfer falling on a bed of sea urchins will take away a painful reminder of the encounter. Avoid wiping out over sea urchins, another example of the benefits of knowing the local area. If you return to shore with broken off spines under your skin, attempt to pull them out carefully without breaking them. Left in, they can cause infection. Soak the affected areas as soon as possible in a solution of hot water and epsom salts, which will aid spine removal and ease pain. If the spines can't be removed, consult a doctor.

Coral. A wipeout leading to a brush with the sharp surface of a coral reef usually produces deep lacerations. The multiple cuts permit the entrance of bacteria. In humid, tropic conditions coral poisoning can result, which is a serious infection. Coral cuts should be treated immediately by washing the wound thoroughly with a mild soap or antiseptic. Healing will be quickened if the wound is allowed to dry. Consult a doctor if infection starts.

If at all possible, avoid walking over coral reefs. They're home to millions of living organisms and are quite fragile. Many tropical reefs are endangered because of human intrusion. When crossing a reef to go surfing, slide on the board as soon as it will float high enough for the fin to avoid hitting the coral.

Sting Rays. Off some sandy beaches, stingrays are a potential hazard. Rays are bottom feeders and often frequent the shallows, but are only a danger if you're wading out. The stingray has a barb on its tail, which is venomous on some species. If stepped on, the ray's tail slashes upward, driving the barb into the foot or ankle. The wound is usually a ragged puncture and very painful. My son, a tough, strong young man, was once spiked by a ray. The pain was so bad he went into shock and had to be helped off the beach. Fortunately, I had just read an article by the "Surf Docs" about emergency treatment for stingray wounds. (Every traveling surfer should take along a copy of the Surfing Medical Association's *Sick Surfers, Ask the Surf Docs and Dr. Geoff Booth,* which you can order from Bull Press; see Resources, page 191.) The Docs recommend immersing the foot in very hot water and soaking the wound for half an hour. During the soak, water as hot as the victim can stand is added. With this treatment, my son's pain quickly subsided and we disinfected the wound. He was surfing the next day.

Jellyfish. Jellyfish can cause a nasty sting. On a surfboard you can spot them before dipping your hands into a tentacle. Jellyfish are quite common in the summer off most North American beaches. The standard first-aid treatment for a sting is to wash the painful area with a dilute solution of ammonia or cover it with a paste made of baking soda and water. In the tropics, and off Australia, some jellyfish, like the Portuguese Man of War, are so venomous that they can be life-threatening. As always, ask the locals before paddling out and when you do go out, be aware.

Surfing's Greatest Hazard

Forget sharks, stingrays, and jellyfish. The greatest danger to surfers today is the one we humans have created. This sea monster has no razor sharp teeth, stinging spines, or lethal tentacles. The danger is usually invisible and a true threat to everyone who enters the sea where the monster lurks. What is it? Water pollution. Surfers get sick when the sea is fouled with sewage and toxic chemicals that spew from industry, big agriculture, and overburdened waste treatment plants. Pollution also comes from the driveways of homes and golf courses that use herbicides and pesticides. Add the road runoff that flows into storm drains after it rains, which also flushes the pesticides, the asbestos, the oil, the heavy metals and the thousand and one harmful chemicals from our urban lifestyle into the sea. This toxic witch's brew of sewage and chemicals has made thousands of surfers and swimmers sick. Ear and stomach infections are rampant off major metropolitan beaches. Lifeguards who enter the water daily near Los Angeles and Santa Monica, California beach storm drains have contracted cancers.

The suspected cause is heavy metal and chemical contamination. Some have died from cancer. Florida's beaches were closed 1,868 times in 1998 due to pollution. Oregon doesn't even test its 360 miles of coastline for health-endangering bacteria and poisons. I temporarily gave up surfing at Malibu's Surfrider Beach because of the bacterial pollution that flows out from the local creek because too many of my friends have become sick from the unhealthy, sewage-contaminated water. For many of us, the sea is our backyard. It becomes fouler each year. We all need to take an active, dedicated stand for the health of the ocean, and our own health as well.

Many beach communities and surfing organizations have organized to fight ocean pollution and improve water quality. There will most likely be one or more activist groups in your area. Seek them out and become involved. In Southern California, the Surfrider Foundation and Heal the Bay (Santa Monica Bay) are leaders in the battle to stop pollution and make the ocean safe for surfers and swimmers.

Heal the Bay (www.healthebay.org) sent a team of environmental investigators to track down the source of pollution making surfers sick at Malibu's Surfrider Beach. They discovered that a sewage plant upstream from Malibu Point was illegally discharging treated sewage into Malibu Creek. With the evidence gathered, the Heal the Bay team obtained a Cease and Desist Order and stopped the discharge. For the time being, the water quality off Surfrider Beach has shown marked improvement.

Surfrider Foundation (www.info@surfrider.org) believes surfers are an "indicator species" of coastal and ocean health; like canaries in a coal mine. The Foundation takes a strong stand to keep the coastal environment healthy. Their "2000/State of the Beach" report is a valuable resource that lets surfers and beach goers have the facts about pollu-

Warning signs are posted for a reason—your health and safety—and should be heeded.
Dixon photos

tion, beach access, erosion, water quality, and surfing areas. The findings, conclusions, and recommendations of this very readable report should be a part of every surfer's library.

Join Surfrider and other similiar groups and help stop polluters, save surfing breaks, and work for a cleaner, healthier ocean.

WAVES
ON LEDGE

Gear

When surfing began in the South Seas centuries ago, all one needed to enjoy sliding was a surfboard. Later, much later, after European contact with the native Hawaiians, came swimming suits. We wear them today because of custom and the protection they offer. Twentieth-century surfers refined the long wooden surfboard and they became lighter, easier to paddle, and caught waves so much better. Until the early 1950s, little else was developed to enhance surfing comfort and safety.

As thousands of surfers became millions worldwide, wave riders with imagination recognized a need for protection against the cold, leashes to keep the surfer connected to the board, and a host of other useful and marketable items. Most of these functional inventions added to the enjoyment of surfing, and allowed more people to ride waves. For some who surfed before the crowds and the sport's growing popularity, leashes, and wetsuits and 10-pound boards ruined surfing.

O'Neill Team Rider Jason "Ratboy" Collins wears a lightweight summer wetsuit. Photo: Dave Nelson. Courtesy: The O'Neill Company

Today you arrive at a surfing spot, take the board from the car's roof rack, slide off the protective cover, check the surf leash, slather sunscreen on your face, wax the board's deck, make sure the nose guard and deck traction pads are stuck down tight, then pull on a wetsuit. After watching the water a while, you take off your UV 400 ultraviolet protecting, polarizing, unbreakable polycarbonate lens sunglasses. If the surf's big and the waves steep and shallow, you might decide to wear a safety helmet, which is also a good idea if the waves are congested. You might don a pair of webbed swim gloves to help your paddling. Then you strap a surf leash to your ankle and head for the waves.

There seems to be no end of surf gear coming on the market, so let's list what most surfers would consider essential gear, and the approximate price range you might find in a typical urban U.S. surf shop—before you ask for a discount. Overseas, expect gear to cost considerably more.

Essentials	Price Range
Surf trunks	$25–$60
Full wetsuit	$150–$300
Summer wetsuit	$85–$125
Leash	$25–$60
Sunglasses (go for quality)	$25–$50
Ding repair kit	$10–$15
Sunscreen	$5–$10
Surf wax	$1

Other Fun and Functional Gear	Price Range
Board cover	$50–$150
Surfboard car rack	$50–$120
Lycra/polypro surf shirt	$30–$50
Surf safety helmet	$65–$100
Deck traction patch	$25–$40
Soft fin for safety	$20–$30
Board nose guard for safety	$10–$15
Webbed gloves for paddling	$15–$30
Ear plugs (protect against infection)	$5–$10

Now we'll go into detail so you can make an educated decision on what surf gear you need for where you usually surf.

Wetsuits

For the first 50 years of modern surfing, wave riders endured the cold or surfed tropical breaks. Today, the great majority of surfers paddle out where ocean temperatures require protection from chilly water. Even in 80° F water, an average person will become chilled after an hour or two. Add a breeze to hasten the evaporation of water on the body and the surfer becomes cold very quickly and begins flirting with hypothermia, with chattering teeth and trembling followed by loss of physical and mental coordination. When this happens, it's almost guaranteed that you'll wipe out on your next wave. These are warnings that the body's core temperature is dropping and hypothermia will soon occur if you don't leave the water and warm up quickly.

Wetsuits, and the surf leash, have greatly extended the range where waves can be ridden. Wetsuits provide needed insulation from the chill,

Corey Lopez wards off Santa Cruz, California, cold water wearing a full wetsuit. Note the traction pads on the tail of his shortboard. Photo: Brian Bielmann. Courtesy: The O'Neill Company

and with tens of thousands of tiny closed cells of inert gas or air within the foam, these synthetic rubber second skins also provide some positive buoyancy. Both qualities can be lifesavers.

Surfers wearing thick neoprene wet suits are riding waves off the Maine coast in winter, along Alaska's frigid shores, and in the freezing water off the Antarctic island of South Georgia. Surf explorer Dr. Mark Renniker, also known by his nickname "Doc Hazard," was the first to surf Alaska and found sliding a wave next to a small iceberg a rather chilling experience. Dr. Renneker also led a group of surfers to the Antarctic. It appears we can surf anywhere swells rise, as long as our wetsuits are thick enough.

Top competitive surfer Rochelle Ballard of Hawaii protects her skin from excess sun and wind chill with a long sleeve Lycra surf shirt. Photo: Brain Bielmann. Courtesy: The O'Neill Company

Wetsuits work by trapping a thin layer of water between the body and the suit. This creates a thermal barrier of warm water—generated by body heat—inside the suit that allows the surfer to function longer in cold seas. This flexible covering of waterproof synthetic rubber, called neoprene, contains thousands of tiny bubbles of air per square yard. These air-filled cells help insulate the skin from the chilling water and slow down the loss of body heat.

Because neoprene is quite flexible and resists the ravages of sun and salt water it makes an excellent wetsuit material. In the early days of wetsuits, both for surfing and skin-diving, the neoprene surface was rough and hard to pull on, especially when wet. Surfers and divers frequently dusted the inside of wetsuit arms and legs with talcum powder to ease getting into the suit. Today, all wetsuits have smooth inner skins that pull on easily. Most have a thin layer of nylon, polyester, or polyproplyene fabric laminated to one or both sides. The polypro-lined wetsuits have become the most popular because of the material's superior insulating properties. As a stretch-fabric polypro liner helps reduce chafing and rash. The wetsuit's slick outer skin sheds water quickly, which reduces evaporative chilling. Some surfers prefer the double-sided fabric coating because the nylon skin resists wear better than non-coated neoprene, even though there is some loss of flexibility and warmth.

A surfing wetsuit's ability to insulate against cold also depends on the thickness of the neoprene. The thinnest material, used in short-leg and shortsleeve suits for summer warm water, is usually two-millimeters thick. Full, extreme-cold-water wetsuits may be as thick as five millimeters. The thicker the material, the more restricted your surfing movements become. If the water's truly cold, you'll need a surf hood, booties, and gloves to prevent heat loss from the head, hands, and feet.

Selecting the Right Wetsuit

Besides a good personal fit, a wetsuit's construction is an important consideration. Like clothes, wetsuits are made by assembling and joining several pieces of neoprene cut from a pattern. The thickness of neoprene allows the seams to be both glued and stitched together. The better the seams are glued and sewn, the longer the wetsuit will last, and the more waterproof it will be. Check that seams are carefully sewn with needle holes that clearly envelop the stitching.

Waterproof seams also increase a wetsuit's insulation factor, but even the most watertight wetsuit can leak if the zipper is not properly waterproofed or if the neckband is too loose. Zippers are hard to waterproof. Most can be sealed with a simple neoprene flap sewn on the inside of the suit that covers the zipper. Finding the proper fit for a neckband is a matter of trial and error. If it's too tight, you'll have trouble breathing: too loose and in comes the cold water. If you plan to surf in waters colder than 60°F, look for wetsuits with sealed seams, since cold water will invade through needle holes. Sealing increases cost, but it also increases the wetsuit's durability.

Wetsuit Types

Wetsuit models range from simple vests to full-body extreme-cold-water suits worn with neoprene booties and hoods. Spring suits might have long legs and short sleeves. Summer suits have short legs, short sleeves, or no sleeves. Then there are "Farmer John" overalls, with long legs and straps that go over uncovered shoulders. Most surfers who surf year around in temperate climates have a full and summer wetsuit. What's best for you will depend on the water temperature you surf in. Keeping warm is important and a big part of enjoying surfing.

How cold water affects you will determine how much protection from the chill you'll need. For the average surfer of average body density, the following is a rough guide to help determine what thickness and type of wetsuit you'll need for temperatures ranging from freezing to warm Tahitian tropical water:

Water temperature (F)	Suit type/thickness
Freezing to 40 degrees	Full dry suit, hood, gloves, booties, thermal polypro underwear
40 to 55 degrees	Full 5mm wetsuit, hood, gloves, booties, thermal polypro underwear
55 to 60 degrees	Full 3mm wetsuit, hood, gloves, booties
65 to 72 degrees	Spring suit, 2mm
73 degrees and up	Surf vest or Lycra shirt

At the minimal end of the wetsuit spectrum are surf shirts and vests. Surf shirts provide some protection from cool water and chilling winds, especially if made from polypro.

Besides giving a bit of insulation from wind chill, surf shirts block the sun's ultra-violet rays, preventing sunburn and surf rash.

Lycra surf shirts help protect the chest from "surf rash," a painful warm-water skin rash that frequently develops after several hours of surfing and paddling. Surf rash is caused by continual abrasive movement of the chest over the waxed deck of the board. A surf shirt also blocks the wind, which will quickly chill you. With your sun block and dark glasses, pack a surf shirt and a thin neoprene vest in your bag when you're traveling to tropic waters.

Selecting a Wetsuit

The most important consideration when buying a new wetsuit is a comfortable fit. Wetsuits come in dozens of shapes, models, and sizes, and each manufacturer cuts from its own patterns, so each wetsuit will fit differently. An O'Neill medium might fit you perfectly, but a Billabong of the same size might be too tight, or a Body Glove a bit loose. The rule here is to try it on before you buy.

Fit should be snug, but not tight. A suit that is too loose, or baggy, will allow too much water to seep inside, reducing its insulating factor.

Extra neoprene under the arms and around the knees may cause chafing and rash. A proper fit allows flexibility, which adds to surfing fun. Some custom-made wetsuits fit so well that very little water enters. It's my guess that the term "wetsuit" evolved because no one could really make them 100% waterproof. I've surfed and dived in dry suits, but unless they're custom fitted they are quite bulky and uncomfortable. Wetsuits are lifesavers and add to the fun of surfing. Buy the best you can afford.

When you're trying on a new wetsuit, make sure you can touch your toes. Then lie on the floor and simulate a paddling motion. Do the arms bind? Next, spring to your feet as if you were standing on your surfboard. Is the suit flexible enough so you can come to your feet quickly and smoothly? Do the zipper or neckband chafe or bind? Then check the fit of wrist and ankle cuffs. These should be tight enough to keep water out but not so snug as to hamper blood circulation. Also check the fit of the kneepads. Some tend to be more flexible than others. If you're a longboarder and knee paddle frequently, the pads will wear more quickly. A wetsuit with Kevlar kneepads would be a good choice.

Wetsuit designs continue to improve with the introduction of new materials. Recently, titanium-laced neoprene and titanium-treated thread have been incorporated into the more expensive, high quality wetsuits. This ultralight, corrosion-resistant metal is supposed to create an effective thermal barrier that reflects body heat. Some wetsuit makers say the use of titanium is high-tech hype and put their emphasis on better fit and flexibility.

Surf shop sales people are quite helpful, since most love the sport. Allow them to make suggestions and assist you in getting a good fit. They want you to be a happy surfer so you'll come back again in two or three years, which is the usual life of an off-the-rack wetsuit if you surf frequently. One warning. Unlike natural rubber or leather, neoprene doesn't stretch over time. So, there's no "breaking in" a wetsuit like a pair of shoes. If you have unusual body proportions, consider having a wetsuit custom made. One made especially for you will cost more, but it will fit properly and add to your enjoyment and safety.

A wetsuit will last longer if you pull it on slowly and gracefully. Try not to stress the seams and zipper. When zipping up, stand upright to avoid undue strain on the zipper. After surfing, use the same caution taking off the wetsuit. Usually the legs are the hardest to pull off. If the wetsuit has your legs in a death grip, simply roll the neoprene downward and then gently peel it off your feet.

Wetsuit Care

You'll probably spend $250 or more for a good, off-the-rack, full wetsuit. That's a big investment that needs proper care to make it pay off.

A few simple steps will help keep your new wetsuit from wearing out before its time. After surfing, fully rinse or soak the suit in fresh water. This dissolves salt and flushes away urine. (Yes, most surfers pee in their suits.) Over time, sunlight will deteriorate the material and fade those colorful panels. Allow the suit to dry in the shade and on both sides. Don't be tempted to use a clothes dryer; the intense heat will destroy the neoprene and void your warranty.

Pulling off the wetsuit along the road or beach usually results in dirt or sand clinging to the neoprene. If the suit gets dirty, wash it with mild detergent and rinse thoroughly. When the suit is fully dry, fold it loosely so the neoprene won't crease. Don't store your wetsuit on a clothes hanger. Over time, the weight of the wetsuit pulling down on the hanger will stretch the neoprene and weaken the shoulder seams. Rips and failed seams can be repaired with neoprene cement that most surf shops sell. You can also buy wetsuit repair kits that come in handy on surfaris. With good care, you can extend the life of your wetsuit a couple of extra years. This saves money and helps the environment. A hundred thousand worn-out wetsuits a year going into a landfill dump pollute. The neoprene manufacturing process also pollutes the atmosphere. By taking good care of your wetsuit, you'll help minimize damage to the environment. Treat your wetsuit like you would your own skin.

Most quality wetsuits are sold with a one-year warranty. If a seam unravels, or some other obvious manufacturing defect occurs, such as the inner fabric delaminating from the neoprene, insist that the warranty be honored. You should keep your sales receipt, warranty card, or both, in a safe place in case you need the suit repaired or replaced.

To keep wetsuits clean when pulling them off on the dirt, some fastidious surfers carry large plastic storage boxes in the back of their vehicles. They'll stand on the box lid while they peel off their surfing skin, then drop the soggy mass of neoprene into the box itself. Don't throw your wetsuit on the roof of the car and, forgetting it's there, drive off.

Surf Leashes

Before surf leashes, a wipeout in large waves usually meant a long swim to shore to retrieve your board, and a lot of surfing time lost swimming. Swimming ability was, and still is, important to surf safely. Most of the big wave, pre–leash era surfers were competitive swimmers, or experienced watermen who had learned to swim well in the ocean. Strapping on a surf leash is no excuse not to learn to swim well.

As surfing's popularity grew, increasing numbers of less-than-proficient swimmers took to the waves. Many who were not skilled watermen became frustrated over having to repeatedly swim after their boards. A few attempted to tie their boards to an ankle, using elastic surgical rubber tubing attached to the board with suction cups. This innovation, developed by Santa Cruz, California, surfer Pat O'Neill, worked in small waves. In medium surf, the rubber tubing either broke or snapped back with such force that the surfer was in danger of being speared by the rocketing board. Some surfers tried bungee cord, but the highly elastic material created the same slingshot effect as surgical rubber tubing.

Around 1975, Santa Monica, California, surfboard maker Con Colburn designed a leash that was strong and with the right amount of elasticity. Colburn's idea was as simple as it was effective. He ran an eight-foot-length of nylon line through a six-foot hollow urethane tube, which limited the stretch to two feet. On one end was a short length of nylon line attached to a tie-down cleat recessed in the board's deck. But how to fix the leash to an ankle so it could be removed quickly in case of emergency? Colburn's production manager, Angelita Miller, designed a comfortable, quick-release ankle strap made from Velcro and neoprene. They named the new leashes "Power Cords," and surfing was changed forever. At first, leashes were called "kook straps"

With rear foot on a tail traction pad this Hawaiian surfer cranks a radical turn. Note his surfleash.

and "real" surfers rejected them wholesale. Within months the leash became an essential part of every surfer's gear.

Today, surf leashes are made of solid urethane cord and come in various lengths and diameters. Short, narrow cords are used on smaller boards. Larger and heavier boards used in big surf require thick, extra-strong cords that can be as long as 15 feet. Again, surf shop sales people can give practical advice in selecting the right cord. It's also a good idea to note what size leash the locals are using where you plan to surf. Expect to pay up to $35 for a high quality leash. Make sure there's a Velcro release where the leash is secured to the board. In an emergency you might have to free yourself from the board at the tail end.

Using the leash is as simple as securing the Velcro strap around whichever ankle faces the rear of the board. Sometimes those long, snakelike cords seem almost alive as they loop around an ankle or catch on a rock. When surfing over coral in shallow water, the leash may snag on an outcropping and pull you off the board into a tangle. Surfers have even caught leash lines on lobster trap buoys. It's a good idea to strap on the leash the same way every time. Then practice freeing the leash with your eyes closed. In an emergency you should be able to free the strap instantly.

There may come a time when you wipe out in the impact zone and your leash hangs up on something. You're caught in an underwater nightmare, tied to your board, which is now flailing about and bashing you, and here comes another set of pounding waves. After a moment of panic, you free the strap as practiced and swim out of danger. Later, when you paddle in, check the cord for cuts. If it's damaged, the leash could snap far offshore, where it's a long swim back to the beach. Most traveling surfers carry a spare leash or two in their board bag.

Surfboard Racks

If you don't own a large SUV, a pickup truck with a long bed, or a station wagon that can swallow a surfboard, you'll need a rack to carry your stick on the top of that coupe or sedan. Racks can be either hard or soft. Hard racks have a rigid bar to which the board is strapped. The rack is attached to the car by means of clamps that hook on the vehicle's rain gutters or door jams. Strong rubber straps are used to hold the board to the rack. Some sort of foam rubber or plastic padding is used to cushion the boards and prevent them from rubbing against the metal bar.

Soft racks are made from strong nylon webbing with clips that are hooked to the car's rain gutter and then tightened by pulling tensioning straps. The portability of soft racks is their best advantage. On a fly-in surf trip, you can carry one with your luggage and any old car can become a surf taxi. Since many newer cars don't have rain gutters, make sure the rack's hold down clips will adapt to the vehicle you'll be using.

Both hard and soft racks work equally well, if care is taken to strap down the board properly. Every time you rack your board check the webbing, adjustment buckles, and hold-down clips. They do wear and corrode. If a strap gives up, you'll probably lose your board and not even be aware that it has blown off the roof. And then there's the person driving behind you swerving aside to avoid your board going through his windshield.

Rack four longboards on a small Toyota or VW Beetle and head down the highway at sixty or seventy miles an hour and you'll experience enough wind resistance to seriously hamper your vehicle's handling characteristics. When I see a small car overtaking me with a pile of boards on top that are held down by an old rusting roof rack, I let them pass and hope to hell those foam and fiberglass missiles stay racked.

Some years back, a surfer friend had a really great board made for him and he wanted to try it out in good surf. We decided to meet at a distant surfing spot for a full day in the waves. He showed up two hours late looking very embarrassed. His old roof rack and new board had blown off the top of his car and he didn't notice their flight until he stopped for gas. Would I help him look for it? The rest of the day we searched along twenty miles of the Pacific Coast Highway and never found his new board. An all-too-obvious lesson was learned that day.

Surfboard Travel Bags

Boardbags are essential if you're a surf traveler or you simply want to protect your board from everyday wear and tear. There's nothing more frustrating than handing over your luggage claim ticket and retrieving a board that's been smashed in transit or dinged by baggage handlers. These days most boards have multiple fins, with some glassed to the board. That's an invitation to serious damage in the cargo hold. Board-bag makers sell hard-foam blocks that shield the fins and tail, protecting them from all but the heaviest blows. It's also a good idea to pad the board, or boards, with bubble wrap or any lightweight shock absorbing material, making sure to double pad the nose and tail.

Some competitive surfers ship their boards in hard cases. Many kinds of boardbags are offered for sale at surf shops. Buy the best you can afford. It's good insurance that your board will survive the long flight to Bali. A tip: Don't put anything hard into the bag that will cause a ding. Wetsuit zippers stuffed into board bags have been known to puncture a surfboard's eggshell-thin fiberglass skin. Make sure your board and case have an accurate identification tag that won't come off in transit. Include all the information necessary to get your board back if it's sent to Sydney and you're going to Fiji. When you buy an airline ticket, ask what it will cost to ship your board. Some international carriers don't charge; others will really sock it to the traveling surfer.

Repair Kits

Dings always happen. On a surf trip a ding-repair kit is a must. Today, resin, catalyst, and fiberglass are combined into a puttylike material that can fill ding holes. The putty hardens when exposed to the sun's ultraviolet rays. When it's hard, the patch material can be sanded smooth. In a pinch, dings can be sealed with industrial quality duct tape—a must in any surf traveler's kit. Serious repair jobs, such as replacing a board's broken-off nose, are best left to surf shop specialists. It's been my observation that beginners botch all but the simplest fiberglass/resin repairs. For major repairs, learn from an expert.

Surfboard Nose and Fin Guards

Nose guards are an essential safety item on pointed surfboards and round nose longboards. These shock-absorbing mini-bumpers are designed to attach on the nose of a board to help protect the surfer and board when they collide. With dagger-point noses being shaped on most short boards, it makes sense to install a nose guard. Your local surf shop will have a do-it-yourself nose guard kit such as SurfCo's easy to install, peel and stick-on nose bumper. A nose guard will also protect your board from dings that have to be repaired, allowing you more time in the water.

In *Surfer* magazine, Richie Collins gave a vivid testimonial for using a nose guard: "I pulled into a tube and it clamped on me. I dove off the end of the board. It hit me in the shin so hard that it broke the nose off in two places inside the nose guard. If I didn't have a nose guard, my shin would have been taken out."

Flexible edge fins serve the same function as nose guards. These fins (skegs), designed and marketed by SurfCo, Hawaii, have soft leading and trailing edges to protect you and other surfers from dangerous encounters with bladelike fins. Surprisingly, many surfers find soft edge fins make a board ride smoother and easier to turn. These Pro Teck flexible leading edge fins have a stiff interior core, which allows

The spear point tips of short boards need soft nose guards to protect the surfers and others. Too many surfers have been hurt needlessly. Surfer Ian Haight uses one just in case. Photo: Steven Bingham Courtesy: SurfCo, Hawaii

Noseguards are made for long and short surfboards. Courtesy: SurfCo, Hawaii

Soft-edged fins are also available for long and short surfboards. Courtesy: SurfCo, Hawaii, Mana Photo

the surfer to make hard bottom turns and cutbacks. Soft edge fins are made for long and shortboards and will insert in most fin box systems. Most surfing injuries occur from nose and fin impacts. Don't take a chance of injuring yourself, or someone else, when a simple soft edge fin and nose guard will offer basic, inexpensive protection.

Surf Wax

For the beginner, a lot of wipeouts are caused by simply slipping off the surfboard's slick deck. A properly applied coat of wax gives very good foot traction. And it's the feet plus body motion that controls the surfboard's direction. It's truly impossible to surf without good traction between surfer and board. Without a dollar bar of surf wax, you'll end slipping and sliding off the board.

Wax every time before paddling out, even if the board has been previously waxed. If the day's warm, wax in the shade. On a hot deck, wax quickly melts and smoothes, losing its traction quality. Soft wax picks up sand like a magnet and does a fine job of sandpapering your skin and wetsuit.

The motion of your skin and wetsuit will also smooth the wax coating. The wax coating can be roughed up with a wax comb, which most surf shops sell or give away if you're buying something. Surf wax is blended for warm or cold water. It's often perfumed, which I hate. There's something sickening about the smell of artificial grape or banana scent wafting off your surfboard. There are even super tacky waxes that competitive surfers prefer, but these can cause skin rash if you're not wearing a wetsuit or Lycra jersey.

Surf wax is available at all surf shops and sold at most markets near surfing areas. Before commercial surf wax, canning paraffin was used and will work in a pinch. A lot of surfers put a half-bar of wax in their trunks and touch up the deck in the water. Surf wax is also a potential heat bomb. Those sticky little bars seem to migrate to washing machines, car carpets, the family clothes washer and dryer, and about anywhere a melted cake can ruin surfaces that don't take kindly to a greasy, platter sized stain that smells of coconut and can't be removed.

Deck Traction Patches

One of the newer innovations which increases a surfer's board control, is a traction patch. These glue-on nonslip deck additions are most often used on the rear decks of shortboards because the surfer's rear foot is usually kept in one spot. Traction pads are applied to the un-waxed deck with waterproof cement. They're available at surf shops in a variety of sizes, shapes and thickness. Most longboard riders pass on deck pads because their feet are constantly moving on the board. Some surfers find traction patches can be abrasive when paddling.

Helmets

An increasing number of surfers are wearing crash helmets, especially in crowded big waves. Like any piece of safety gear, try it on and test it for comfort and fit before you buy. Surf helmets should be worn snug. Some have transparent visors that pull down from the helmet and shield the eyes from spray. My son likes to wear a helmet when he surfs areas with lava or coral bottoms because of the protection they give during a wipeout. In the future, surf helmets may become mandatory in competitive events. It may be that surf armor will be the trendy surf statement of tomorrow. With surf gear, use what works for you, but don't be a slave to fashion.

In big waves or small, a surf safety helmet offers added protection from a collision or wipeout. Surfer Mitch Thorson grabs a wild wave at Margaret River, Western Australia. Courtesy: Gath Sports Pty. Ltd.

Young grommet Yadin Nickle, Margaret River, Australia, comes off the lip of a small, fast-breaking wave. Courtesy: Gath Sports Pty. Ltd.

The Big Surf

Big wave–surfing means different things to different surfers. To the men and women who ride the huge surf off Hawaii's North Shore it means the powerful waves that roll in at Sunset Beach, Makaha, and Waimea Bay. In California, big surf means a ten-foot day at Steamer Lane, Santa Cruz, or an eight-foot south swell at Malibu. On the East Coast, six-foot waves breaking off Cocoa Beach, Florida, or at Ditch Plains, on New York's Long Island, are considered huge by the locals.

For most recreational surfers, overhead waves are big waves. The main difference between big surf and small, of course, is size and immense power, and what a bad wipeout could do to you. Big waves break with a fearsome intensity that places great demands on a surfer's skill and physical conditioning. Then there's the surfer's mental attitude. Without confidence, backed up by big wave experience, surfing the heavies can be deadly.

Surfers of truly big waves are one hundred percent committed athletes. Riding big waves is a career and a lifestyle. A few make a

Flea Virostki drops where others would not dare at Mavericks.

respectable living surfing the giants by allowing their reputation and image to be linked to surf products. One of the modern pioneer California big wave–surfers, Jeff Clark, was the first to ride the awesome waves of Mavericks, off Santa Cruz, California, and from 1975 to 1989 Jeff surfed these huge, cold-water waves by himself. Mavericks was his turf, and he gave the place its worldwide reputation. Later, Jeff trademarked the word "Mavericks," which seems a reasonable action after he had risked his life for so many years.

It's my guess that around the world's oceans there are fewer than one hundred surfers who are truly qualified in body and mind to consistently, and safely, handle huge waves in the twenty-foot-and-up class. The best big wave–surfers are a rare breed. They all have great courage, backed up by enormous skill and years of experience in the water. They know the art and craft of surfing in depth.

Doctor Mark Renneker, an internist from San Francisco, is a perfect example of a big wave–rider who knows his way around the world's prime surfing spots. "Doc Hazard," as his surfing friends call him, is pushing 50 years old, but year after year he'll find time to surf the world's largest waves. Mark's first a brilliant doctor, but he understands waves and surfboards as well as he does his patients' medical problems. He's surfed the best and biggest waves from Alaska to Fiji to

Five-time world champion Kelly Slater races down the face of a Mavericks giant.

Chile and points south. With all his experience, he knows when it's time to back off. I had the good pleasure of attending two Surfers' Medical Association (SMA) conferences with Mark on Tavarua Island, Fiji—the home of perhaps the world's best reef break. On a day of huge waves, we were in the Tavarua surf taxi approaching an offshore surfing reef named Cloudbreak. Mark stared at the thundering swells exploding over the coral and murmured, "You know, gang, a guy could get hurt out there. Let's come back later."

Of course, we all agreed with Doc Hazard's sage observation. None of us really wanted to leave the safety of the boat for what could have been a very dangerous, even disastrous, surf session.

What follows is meant to discourage you from paddling out into what could be the most dangerous experience in your life. If you must challenge huge waves, then be prepared to spend years becoming qualified. Above all, you must become a waterman or waterwoman to ride the big surf. For every person rescued in big waves, someone puts their life on the line. So, please think twice, and then again, before putting yourself and others in peril.

Some surfers measure huge waves not in feet, but in increments of fear. This fear concept came from pioneer North Shore big wave–rider Peter Cole. Wave height is always difficult to measure, especially if

133

you're in the trough and paddling up the face of a giant breaker about to pitch out and bury you. At those decisive and fearful moments, it's understandable to judge a wave to be higher than it actually is. Wave height is not as important as what the wave does to the attitude of the surfer. To some, a lazy five-footer looks huge and scary. To experienced surfers, huge waves are frightening only when they lose control. Control of your board, your fatigue, and your mental state are the three basics of surviving in big surf. When you lose control, the wave usually wins—and the punishment starts. Big waves weigh hundreds of tons and can roll in at twenty-five miles per hour. The surfers who ride the moving mountains of Oahu's North Shore were not natural born big wave riders, though many grew up there watching big wave surfing. They all went through a surfer's apprenticeship—years of paddling, progressing from small waves to large, crushing wipeouts, learning to judge waves, and how to survive killer wipeouts, until at last came the day they paddled down the face of a truly big wave.

Tow-in Surfing

How big is big? Truly big surf, in the 50- to 80-foot-from-trough-to-crest range, is now being ridden by surfers towed into the wave by personal watercraft (PWCs—otherwise known as "Wave Runners" or "Jet-Skis"). Because no human has the strength to paddle a board fast enough to achieve takeoff speeds on these monster offshore swells, surfers came up with the idea of using a motorized assist, and tow-in surfing evolved.

Since the mid-1990s the men and women who tow-in into these giants have become the superstars of the surfing world, thanks to magazine and media coverage. The outer reef breaks where they ride these awesome waves—Jaws off Maui, Mavericks north of Santa Cruz, California, Todo Santos in Mexico, and Tahiti's Teahupoo—are the world's ultimate giant wave, tow-in surfing spots. As monster wave–surfing expands, and it will because of its limitless challenge and death-or-glory appeal, surfers will discover other giant deep water breaks.

A hundred miles off the Southern California coast an underwater mountain thrusts upward, just breaking the surface. In January 2001, a group of four big wave–surfers anchored off the Cortez Banks to attempt riding these monster waves. This offshore tow-in surfing expedition was conceived in 1991 by trip leader Larry Moore. Several times from an airplane Moore had watched giant open-ocean swells roll over Cortez Banks and rise dramatically to become, what Moore believed, ridable waves. What the four surfers found on their dawn arrival were perfect 30- to 50-foot waves. The surf was so big that it showed clearly on the support boat's radar. Better yet, the wind velocity was zero and

A typical gnarly Mavericks wave, only to be ridden by surfers ready for the challenge. A wave like this took Mark Foo's life.

These outer reef breaks would be impossible to surf without a motorized takeoff assist.

the seas were glassy calm. For two days the four surfers had fantastic rides of 400 yards and more on giant, well-formed waves. The rides were faster than any of the veteran big wave–surfers had ever experienced. They easily kept up with their partner's tow-in jet-skis, which were cruising at 30 mph.

The question now is what comes next with tow-in surfing? So far, no one has been killed on these giant wave tow-in surfing expeditions, but it's only a matter of time until this compulsive drive to push the limits does take a life.

Tow-in surfing pioneers like Ken Bradshaw, Brian Keaulana, Laird Hamilton, Darrick Doerner, and Dave Kalama put their lives on the line to develop relatively safe ways to ride giant outer reef waves. All these surfers had decades of big wave surfing experience before they attempted to be towed into Jaws or other offshore breaks. They learned by trial and error how to handle their big wave tow-in boards (7½ feet × 17 inches × 2 inches and 35 pounds), which feature foot straps, while being whipped into a wave for a 30 mph takeoff. At these speeds, and with the wind created by the wave, it's all too easy to get airborne, especially if the face is choppy. Going airborne means taking the big drop and a horrendous wipeout.

Purists criticize the use of powered watercraft in surfing. Some say being towed into a wave is like having a snowmobile or helicopter haul a mountain climber up Mount Everest. There are also environmental and aesthetic concerns. The two-cycle gas engines powering these PWCs spew out a lot of unburned gasoline and oil that fouls the water. When that slippery, toxic stuff gets on your surfboard, or in your mouth after a wipeout, you have a right to protest, and maybe more. Then there's the scream of high-pitched engines overpowering the sound of the surf. Both types of pollution can ruin a perfect day for paddle-in surfers.

Perhaps there might be a compromise: No tow-in, gasoline-powered assists where paddle-in surfers are catching waves. Period.

Despite these objections, tow-in surfing is here to stay. Look, for example, at the surf fashion business pushing tow-in surfing to create image, which sells everything. The men who pioneered and perfected this dramatic variation of surfing are well aware of their PWCs' polluting nature. To counter these objections, they point out that hundreds of lives have been saved by beach lifeguards using PWCs. Fine, some say, let only lifeguards use them and keep surfing pure and simple. The outer-reef surfers stress that very few people tow-in and that their big-wave surfing takes place far offshore. That's now. In the future will those remote big-wave breaks experience "Wave Runner" traffic jams? Will waterborne cops sort out the congestion as lifeguards race wipeout and collision victims back to shore and waiting ambulances?

Going Big

Tow-in or paddle-in big wave–surfing is eminently dangerous. Recently four experienced big wave–riders lost their lives in giant surf. During the winter of 1997 Todd Chesser, a veteran big wave–rider, drowned surfing an outside reef off Oahu's North Shore. The day was perfect. The waves were in the 15-foot range, the sea was glassy, and Chesser and two friends were looking forward to classic big waves. Before they paddled out a Civil Defense official had warned Chesser and his companions to expect huge surf later in the day. His prediction was accurate. A set of 30-foot rogue waves rolled out of the horizon. Before the three surfers could paddle to safety, they were caught inside the break and hammered against the bottom. Todd did not survive.

A year later to the day, big wave–surfer Donnie Solomon drowned at Waimea Bay. An accident at an outer-reef break called Phantom's took the life of Jim Broach the same season.

Mark Foo's death in the winter of 1995 at Mavericks, California's premiere big-wave break, shook the surfing world. Mark was a great all-around surfer, with 10 years of extensive experience in big waves, but he had yet to ride Mavericks. To challenge Mavericks when the waves are really going off is every top surfer's dream. The cold water

Photographers watching surfers fighting to paddle out at Waimea Bay. Not a good spot to be caught inside.

and rocks, wild surging currents, and the ominous feel of the usually overcast area make it a scary place to surf.

Mark was a professional surfer and he needed to include Mavericks on his big-wave resume. When he received word that Mavericks was "all time," he and Ken Bradshaw caught the overnight flight from Hawaii to San Francisco. By 11 o'clock the next morning, fresh from the warm seas of Hawaii, Mark and Ken were paddling out in numbing 52-degree water encased in thick, heavy-duty wetsuits.

What happened next is still unclear. A strong set of 15-footers roared into Mavericks and Mark and Bradshaw paddled down the face of one of them. Bradshaw was on the inside, saw the wave was going critical, and backed off. Mark Foo kept paddling and stood. Halfway down the wave's face he lost his balance, pitched forward and was buried by the wave.

Moments later, other surfers were taking off and getting in serious trouble. Not one of the dozens of surfers, camera boat people, or those watching from the beach realized that Mark Foo had not surfaced after his critical wipeout. Most thought that Mark's board had snapped in half and he had left the water to get his spare. Some ninety minutes passed before his body was spotted and recovered. How did this terri-

Someone must have yelled 'Outside!' to cause this whole group to begin paddling seaward to safer water.

ble tragedy happen? He may have hit the bottom, or perhaps was hit by his board. His leash might have become snared on rocks. To this day, no one really knows, but some lessons were learned. Mark had no previous experience surfing Mavericks, and he was probably tired from his overnight flight from Hawaii. Proud and driven, he may have let his desire to join the Mavericks crew overcome the need to rest and thoroughly check out the spot. Whatever the cause, his death points out the stark reality that big wave–surfing is very dangerous and only for the highly experienced.

Most surfers will never experience outer-reef tow-in surfing or charge down the face of a gnarly Mavericks or Waimea giant, but many will at some point paddle out to where wave size becomes frightening and survival may be in doubt. Waves awesome enough to get your adrenaline pumping and start you asking, "What the hell am I doing out here?" need to be respected and approached with caution.

What's so different about big waves except for their size? Speed and raw power. A big wave has the destructive capacity of a major landslide or avalanche. Imagine what would happen if a 30-foot wave collapsed on a typical wooden beach house. Splinters. On a big, steep wave you'll surf faster than you ever thought possible. The sheer volume of water in a huge incoming swell indicates that the wave is carrying a tremendous store of energy. Because of wave size, the surfer develops tremendous speed on the takeoff, which is good because you need speed to outrace the breaking shoulder or the wave's lip cresting above you.

In bigger surf you plan a couple of moves ahead. Your turns are wider, longer, and more flowing. On a big wave you'll *really* work to carve a turn, and your legs do most of the labor. You'll encounter excessive gravitational forces as you bottom-turn. Some surfers say you'll feel a downward pull of two to three G's. So many physical demands and unusual sensations hit the big-wave rider at once it's a wonder that they can deal with the sensory overload. There will be choppy rough water on the wave's face that causes the board to chatter. Winds come gusting suddenly from nowhere and threaten to blow you off the board. Then there's the sound of all that roaring, cascading water trying to take you down.

Confidence is everything in surfing. Successful big wave–surfers have a positive attitude about paddling out and going for the heavies. A belief in yourself, backed up by experience and the skills you've acquired, goes a long way in overcoming one's normal and healthy fear of big surf. If you're physically and mentally ready for big surf, and believe you can make the wave, most of the time you'll pull it off.

Mavericks pioneer Jeff Clark had this to say about that awesome California cold-water winter break: "Big wave–surfing becomes dangerous when people get pushed into situations where they don't

A classic closeout wave at Sunset Beach, Oahu, and every surfer has abandoned ship. Photo: Dr. Don James from Peter Dixon collection

belong. You have to know your ability, and that just comes from experience. You have to do your homework."

It's important to ask yourself what drives you out there to the
lineup. Is it peer pressure? Your ego? Machismo? Or a strong belief
that you're ready for the challenge and will accept the risks. If it's the
latter, your chances of returning to the beach stoked and confident
with some big-surf experience behind you will be greatly increased.

Survival in Big Surf

For some surfers, big waves may be anything over five feet; for others,
20-footers are warmup waves. Generally, overhead surf has the power to
cause problems paddling out, wiping out, and getting back to the beach.
Even if you never surf the heavies, here are the basics of catching, riding—and surviving—in big waves that most experienced surfers would
agree on:

- Know your limitations. Don't paddle out if you have any doubt
  about your ability, strength, or mental state.

Not the biggest, but every double overhead wave has the potential for a hold-down.

- Study the break and how the guys in the lineup are surfing it. Look for channels, ripcurrents, deep and shallow spots, rocks and reefs, and other hazards.

- Check out who is catching, and making, the most waves. Learn from the stars.

- Time the intervals between sets of incoming swells and the waves themselves. You need to know approximately when to expect the arrival of the next big set, and how many waves it may contain, so you won't get caught inside the break.

- Use a surfboard that's long and stable enough for the waves you'll be facing. A board between 10 and 11 feet long is needed, depending on your size. Longer boards paddle faster and may keep you out of trouble. Again, check out what the local big wave riders are using.

- Use an extra strong big-wave leash like the locals are using. Some surfers use 20 feet of cord. Shorter leashes can be tied together if necessary.

- Make sure you know where the waves are not likely to break, so you won't be buried by an avalanche of churning whitewater while paddling out.

It takes a really big Waimea Bay wave face to support three surfers.

- Keep an eye out on your companions. Big-wave riders watch out for each other; in big surf everyone is a lifeguard. Learn CPR; it can be done in the water if you know how.

- Stick a swim fin in your wetsuit or trunks in case you find yourself caught in a rip or swept far offshore.

Getting Out

It's time to go for what you've longed to do and trained hard so hard for. If you truly feel you're ready for big waves, paddle out for the lineup. Once outside, you'll be low surfer in the pecking order, but with good humor and patience your wave will come.

Once you get past the shorebreak, take your time paddling out. Stay in the channel or paddle around the breaking area. *Never* get caught in front of the surfers riding in. If you do, you'll endanger both them and yourself. Paddling out to the lineup should be a warmup. Conserve your energy, and most important, don't get winded. You'll need all your strength and wind for critical moments, like catching a wave or surviving a bad wipeout and the subsequent hold-down. As always, keep your head up and eyes on the horizon. The sooner you see a set of big ones rolling in, the quicker you can make a decision about what to do next. Some surfers, as they paddle over the top of a swell, stand so they can better see what's approaching and decide what to do next. Next might be to paddle faster and get outside where the waves are not breaking, or to head quickly for deeper water. Each decision carries its rewards and penalties.

Watch the locals and do what they do. If the furthest surfer outside the lineup starts paddling frantically for the horizon you'll know a big set is coming. Now you're in real trouble. You decide to head for the channel and deeper water in hopes the swells won't break there. They don't. You make it outside to the lineup. Now you can slow down and get your breath. After a brief pause, paddle farther out to where it would be very unlikely for a wave to crest and get some more rest. When the time comes to go for a big wave, you must be energized.

Caught Inside

At some point you will get caught inside as a big set rolls in. You'll paddle over two or more waves and then suddenly one will come that leaps up and pitches out. There's no way to get over the crest before it breaks. The wave is going critical and it's too late to duck dive. It's bailout time. As you abandon ship, shove the board as far to the side as possible, so it will roll like a log rather than being snapped in half by the wave's impact. Pushing the board away reduces the chance of you colliding with it. This also extends the leash, which stops it from coiling around you or your board. Surfers have had their leashes snare them around the neck. Not a happy experience in a bad wipeout.

While there's time, take as many breaths as possible and supercharge your blood with oxygen. Just before you head for deep water to escape the wave's impact, suck in a full breath and fill your cheeks with air. That tiny extra bit of air might give you 10 seconds more consciousness before passing out. Don't dive too deep. You don't want to stay under any longer than necessary or impact the bottom. Keep your eyes open underwater. You may become so disoriented that you'll need to look for daylight to decide which way is up. You can also see areas where water boils for the surface. Sometimes it's possible to ride an upwelling to the top. With eyes open you'll spot coral heads or rocks in time to avoid smashing into them. Use your arms to protect the head from the board or rocks, or to prevent the leash from looping around your throat and becoming a noose. A hold-down can be punishing. A beat-down is always brutal. In either case, relax and go with the flow. Conserve your wind and energy for the swim to the surface. When you see and sense that the wave has passed, swim all out for daylight. Pop up and look seaward before you breathe. You don't want to exhale and then suck in a lungful of foam, a sometimes-fatal mistake that causes uncontrollable coughing fits. If it's safe to breathe, start rapidly charging your body with oxygen. There may be another wave bearing down on you. And look out for your board. If it's pulling on your ankle, at least you know where it is. If not, the board could be anywhere. Protect your head and face by putting up your arms to block the board.

You've survived a closeout wave. Now climb back on the board and paddle out to the channel. You'll probably be scared and exhausted. So work out to where you know the waves won't be breaking and recharge your physical and emotional batteries. Or if the surf seems all too much, paddle in before getting hurt—or worse.

Catching Big Waves

The locals will appreciate you letting them have the best waves and not getting in their way. After a while they may even notice that you haven't got in their way, and that you respect older surfers and female waveriders, and that you occasionally compliment someone on a great ride. In time, this submissive behavior will prompt someone to nod or say your turn has come. When that golden moment arrives, make the most of it by going all out.

The crowd in the lineup is always intimidating, though they may not intend to be. You have three choices to position yourself:

1) Work your way to the most critical point in the lineup and wait for that moment when everyone else backs off. Now, go for the wave. You'll likely wipe out, but the others surfers will respect your aggro attempt.

2) Wait for the surfers to signal that it's your wave. That could happen where it's not crowded.

3) Hang out off to the side of the lineup and wait for a swell to swing wide in your direction. You might be the only person in position for the takeoff.

It's the big decision time. You're fully rested now and have paddled closer to the takeoff zone. By now, you've learned never to take your eyes off the horizon. Off to the side a friendly, experienced surfer calls out, "First time, right?"

You nod.

"I'll keep an eye on you, you do the same for me. Okay?" says friendly surfer.

A late takeoff too close together at Sunset Beach, Oahu, means an almost certain wipeout.

"Deal, and thanks."

You found somebody that cares. Your confidence soars. An hour or two passes. Everyone's catching waves but you. Patience. Then someone warns excitedly, "Outside!"

A set rolls in and it's not too big. Everyone glances at each other. You look around. They're all waiting for you to make a move. It's time. You want a wave badly, bad enough to throw caution aside and risk your life. You spin the board to face shore and begin paddling. At the same time, drawing in lungful after lungful of air to saturate your blood with oxygen. You sense the wave rising up behind you. The tail of the board goes up and the nose points down into the trough. All the while you're paddling hard. You keep paddling, harder and harder. The board begins sliding sharply downward and there's no pulling out. Now it's only you and the wave. You take five more strokes and come to your feet in a balanced power crouch. Rocketing down the face of the wave, you accelerate to maximum speed. Near the trough you make the bottom turn, pushing down hard on your inside rail and accelerating away from the breaking peak. Your speed is so great that you begin to climb up the face. Picking your best line of attack, you trim the board for stability, race across the face, and grab a couple of deep breaths. The wave holds and you sense you've made this one. Out on the shoulder you judge if there's time for a cutback. You turn toward the breaking shoulder, decide not to chance a wipeout, and cut back. You surf on, grinning now, until the wave begins to flatten. After kicking out, paddle for the channel and the safety of deeper water. Rest, catch your breath, and paddle back to the line up.

Yes, it was crazy, but the exhilaration and sense of accomplishment far outweigh the hazards. Your fingers tremble slightly and you're breathing hard. Everything your eyes take in seems extra brilliant and in greater detail. It was pure fun and a peak experience. Now, it's time for another wave and another chance for a wipeout.

Big-Wave Wipeouts

After a severe wipeout some surfers give up the big waves. They discovered their limitations, or hadn't trained enough for the physical and emotional demands of double-overhead and higher surf. The big-wave riders who successfully survive huge waves and horrendous wipeouts, year after year, have all made a total lifestyle commitment. They live where the big swells arrive and know the wave environment intimately. The rewards from their dedication to surfing are certain fame, and for some, an unsure income. But the real reward for most is being in the waves among the few elite surfers who dare put their lives on the line to enjoy one of the most enriching and intense experiences our planet offers. Whether the surf is large or small, the real joy is in simply catching a wave. When you've done it, you'll be just that much more alive.

So you're out there. Don't sweat it. No matter how cautious or skilled you are in big surf, you will wipe out. Here are some basic guidelines for handling big-wave wipeouts:

Being mentally prepared for a wipeout begins with your physical training. Everyone who paddles out to challenge big surf must be a strong swimmer and paddler. The ability to hold one's breath underwater is especially important in a long hold-down. The great surfers train hard, and a lot of them train themselves specifically in breath-holding. In a pool, or calm water, practice swimming underwater while holding your breath. Always have someone along to watch you. It's all too easy to reach a point of oxygen depletion and pass out, and each of us has a threshold. Anoxia comes very quickly and with little warning once the level of oxygen in the blood drops to a low level. I've passed out twice underwater. The first time was on a movie job when my safety diver failed to leave a bottle of air where I could reach it in an emergency. Something went wrong and I passed out trying to swim up from an underwater movie set. The cameraman no-

Davey Miller, struggling for the surface after a long hold-down wipeout.

ticed I was missing and went back underwater. He found me on the bottom unconscious. I had felt an intense craving for air, then came fear, followed by a feeling of detachment, and my focus shifted to little star bursts of light in my brain. That's all I remembered until waking up on the surface.

The second incident occurred while I was night-diving for lobster, when a wave jammed me into a rock cave. I went through the same stages: the craving for air, the fear and detachment, the bright brain lights. I somehow floated out of the cave and came to the surface beside the small boat my wife was rowing. She shipped the oars and said with a note of worry, "You were down a long time."

In neither case did I panic during these very near-drownings. During both incidents I kept my mouth and throat sealed, and no water entered my lungs. Fortunately, I was an experienced waterman and knew that opening my lips would likely be the end. What I experienced is called "dry drowning." I was in top physical condition, a competitive swimmer and skin-diver, and had an attitude that I would survive at all costs. The surfer in a bad wipeout must be prepared to hold his breath underwater to the point of unconsciousness and beyond. Frequently the buoyancy of a wetsuit, or the surfboard attached

The Pipeline claims another board. One of the realities of big-wave surfing. This is a classic 1967 shot. Dr. Don James from the Peter Dixon Collection.

to an ankle by the surfer's leash will bring an unconscious person to the surface, where a designated buddy may save the victim.

When that super-critical wipeout does happen, knowing that you can hold your breath for a couple of minutes and longer will give you the confidence to carry on the fight to survive. Some big wave–surfers emotionally detach themselves from the emergency by slowly counting the seconds they're underwater. They report seeing themselves from an external point of view during the long hold-down. This self-created psychological distance from your immediate peril certainly helps control panic. Since most wipeout hold-downs rarely go beyond 30 seconds, it's reassuring to know that you can go without breathing for two minutes and longer. The calmer you stay, the less you panic and struggle, the longer your oxygen will last. And that additional air in your puffed out cheeks may give you an extra few seconds of consciousness. When the moment comes to make your break for air and daylight, be decisive and fight upward for all your worth.

When you go down in a deep-water break, the only real danger is being hit by your board. As you wipe out, try to dive into and through the wave to escape going over the falls. If you do take a long, out-of-control fall down the wave's face, you'll get held under for sure, and that can be terrifying, especially on your first big wave wipeout. You'll

The speed and raw power of big waves offer little room for mistakes. Dixon photo

surface, make sure it's safe to grab air, then duck under as the next wave cascades down on you. Big wave–surfers do survive hold-downs that last for two and three waves. You can too, if you've trained for that possibility.

You'll be dragged along by your board and leash. That's okay. Go with the flow of the whitewater toward shore. Relax; don't fight all that force, and let the wave carry you until its power abates. When you're released from its grip, paddle into the channel and catch your breath.

If you want to go in to the beach, stay away from the middle of the channel, where the water usually flows seaward. Look for the shoreward flow that feeds into the channel and allow it to help carry you ashore.

A wipeout over a reef break is another story. Swells that power in to become surf over a shallow reef usually break hard and fast. When you wipe out over a reef, like the Pipeline, the bottom is right there waiting for you. The bottom may be jagged coral or gnarly, barnacle-covered rocks. Most experts agree that it's wise to stay in the wave as long as possible. An early bailout results in the full force of the wave driving you under. When you do get driven down, it's a good idea to take a fetal position and wrap your head in your arms.

CHAPTER
Eight

Bodysurfing

Bodysurfing provides a certain spiritual thrill that must be experienced to be understood. Riding almost to shore on the shoulder of a six-foot wave can lift you like nothing else. It's a pure-and-simple, no-hype sport that gives you great boisterous good fun.

Bodysurfing, to purists, is the ultimate way of achieving oneness with the sea. Literally, there's nothing separating the bodysurfer from the wave. When the takeoff and ride all come together for a long rush along the tumbling face of a breaker, it's a total emotional and physical high. It's also one of the easiest surf sports to learn, if you can get the "feel" of what's required. There is also a link between stand-up surfing and bodysurfing. The two are similar, and each requires surf knowledge and an understanding of wave dynamics. Become skilled in one and you'll be better at the other.

To bodysurf well you need to develop an intuitive sense for the individual wave you're trying to catch. Once you've mastered the basic skills, bodysurfing becomes a truly exhilarating experience.

Running the tube at The Pipeline. Photo: M.M. Kliks

Best of all, sliding a wave with only your body can be enjoyed almost anywhere waves break from a foot high to ten feet and more. With an outlay for swim fins and trunks you're fully equipped to start sliding waves. Where the water's chilly, add a wetsuit. Can you think of any other active sport, besides running, that requires less gear and expense?

One day at Venice Beach, California, when the surf was huge and perfect for bodysurfing, and a lot of us were getting long angling rides, one of the pumped swimmers remarked, "Man, this must be the closest thing to the trauma of being born."

On a business trip to Portugal some years ago, before traveling surfers discovered that the Portuguese coast had excellent surf, I packed a pair of swim fins in case I found ridable waves. Just north of Lisbon, I spotted a long concrete jetty thrusting into the Atlantic. Peeling off the seawall were perfect bodysurfing waves. As the incoming swells rolled against the seawall they began to break with steep, curling shoulders that, with the help of fins, could be caught. After watching the waves for 20 minutes and looking for possible hazards, I trotted out to the end of the jetty and jumped off. When you don't know what the bottom's like, or the depth, it's best not to dive in. With swim fins I was able to reach takeoff speed on these tunneling beauties and body-

Straight off bodysurfing on a perfect spilling wave. Cecil Charles took this classic photo back in 1938 while hanging from the Santa Monica Pier. Photo: Peter Dixon Collection

surfed alongside the jetty for nearly 100 yards. What a thrill. I caught wave after wave, until cold and exhaustion drove me back to the beach. Then I noticed the crowd. Dozens of people had gathered, and several curious young men fingered my swim fins and asked questions in Portuguese. Using hand motions to overcome the language barrier, I was able to describe the process of catching a wave by sliding down its moving face.

Fins

Swim fins are among the best water tools invented. With the extra thrust provided by pair of fins, an average swimmer suddenly becomes a college-level sprinter. The idea was so simple. Attach a pair of flexible rubber, fishlike tail fins to one's feet to increase thrust and kick hard. That's what Owen Churchill, the inventor of swim fins, did in the late 1930s quite successfully. His innovative swimming aid was quickly adopted by skin-divers, who were the first to realize the advan-

153

Bodysurfer getting ready for an underwater takeoff using duckfoot fins.

tage of fins—and a new aquatic sport was born. After World War II, a small number of people who bodysurfed began pulling on fins and riding waves. Fins, like the Boogie Board, have helped draw millions of people into the fun and soul satisfaction the ocean gives us all.

My afternoon bodysurfing session surfing off Lisbon has become a cherished memory, and it wouldn't have happened without those old Churchill fins. Ever since, when I'm planning to travel anywhere near a body of water, I take swim fins. I've also used my fins several times to make ocean rescues that would have been quite dangerous without the extra swimming power they gave. Truly, fins are lifesavers, and a growing number of beach lifeguards are using fins for rescues.

Fins make bodysurfing in over-the-head depths possible. Without the thrust and speed fins provide, even a strong swimmer will have trouble catching a wave.

A few observations from using fins for longer than I care to remember: Select fins for their intended purpose. Heavy, stiff, long bladed scuba-diver fins are not suitable for bodysurfing. Only two types work well in the surf. Look for either Churchill or Duckfoot fins, which have become the bodysurfers' fin of choice. Both types are supposed to float if you lose one, but I've discovered that when fins get old they lose buoyancy and sink. Both have straps that pull over the heel. If they fit well, either will provide ample thrust. My all-time favorites were soft, no chafing, pure gum rubber Duckfeet. Since gum rubber is no longer available, I prefer Churchills because of their comfort. There are many brands of swim fins from which to choose on the market today; remember it's comfort that is the most important consideration in selecting bodysurfing fins. If fins don't fit well, they'll cause blisters or cramps. If they're too loose, your fins will surely be ripped off in a pounding, tumbling wave.

Like buying a good pair of shoes, try the fins on before you hand over your $35 to $75. To prevent cramping and chafing, the foot pocket should have enough room for your toes. Heel straps should feel a bit snug. Check the straps that pull over the heels for rough spots that would rub and blister the skin. The fin blade should be flexible, but not floppy. I'm fortunate that Churchill's medium-large fins fit me perfectly, so I stick with them. You might find other types are better suited for your feet. A good pair of fins should last eight to ten years if they're kept out of the sun when not in use. When fins age, the heel straps will begin to show signs of cracking and it won't be long until the strap breaks. When cracks appear, replace your fins.

Big-wave bodysurfers often use fin keepers, extra straps of strong nylon webbing that help secure fins to your ankles and ensure that they don't get ripped off in blasting wipeouts. Most have Velcro fasteners that allow the straps to be adjusted for comfort. Fin keepers are sold in almost every surf and dive shop. They're a good investment if you bodysurf in pounding waves.

The Bodysurf Wave

The seven summers I worked as a beach lifeguard, I watched thousands of people hurl themselves shoreward in collapsing waves attempting to bodysurf. Most, no matter how hard they tried, didn't have a clue about how to catch a wave with their body.

Beginners get blasted and buried repeatedly by crashing sandbusters. A few get hurt or need to be rescued. Somewhere out in the surf will be people who do know how and their tumultuous slides down the face of a spilling wave make it look so easy. It is, if you know how.

Like board surfing, the whole trick to bodysurfing is picking the right wave, then putting yourself in the best spot to start the slide down the wave's face. In chest-deep water you can simply push off the bottom, take a stroke, angle downward, and you're a bodysurfer. In deeper water you'll need fins to provide thrust. With a hard stroke or

Bodysurfing these pounding sandbusters would not be wise. Dixon photo

two, and a strong kick, you'll start the downward slide. The most important move is positioning your head and shoulders lower than your hip and legs. That's it in brief. Now for the details.

Bodysurfing can be enjoyed at almost any ocean beach where swells build with sufficient strength and height to produce spilling surf. Even waves a foot high will allow a slide, but the fun begins in three-foot and up surf. A few highly skilled and waterwise bodysurfers have ridden waves of 20 feet. Beginners should stick to waves in the one to three-foot range. Anything larger has too much power for a new bodysurfer to handle. A few minutes of wave watching will suggest the best areas to ride. Avoid pounding, close-to-shore breaking sandbusters that dump violently in shallow water. Of course, there are lulls between sets of waves. These brief periods of calm seem to draw beginners seaward, but usually not far enough to be outside the break. Then comes another big set of waves and they're caught in the impact zone. Blam! And the lifeguards sprint to the rescue.

Most novice bodysurfers don't realize that beaches that drop off sharply to deep, over-the-head water will cause waves to break closer to shore. Large, crashing shorebreak waves can be very dangerous. Pounding sand busters can break bones, dislocate shoulders, and even smash the unwary unconscious. Strong ripcurrents can carry swimmers far beyond where they should be. The best and safest novice bodysurfing beaches are characterized by a gradually sloping bottom where the breaking waves spill from top to bottom instead of dumping all at once. These gradually descending beaches allow the swimmer to wade out some distance from shore to the breaking surf, giving a longer ride. Again, if the wave rises up steeply and breaks violently close to dry sand, it's a crashing bone-buster that should be avoided.

The larger the wave, the farther it will break from the beach and the longer the ride. Wave-watching will also reveal possible hazards such as submerged rocks, floating objects, and ripcurrents. These dangers are covered in chapter 5. Offshore sandbars will also help a swell rise to become ridable surf. As mentioned, jetties, piers, and rocky points often produce good bodysurfing waves, though each present hazards of sharp rocks and barnacle-encrusted pilings.

Look for waves that spill downward from their crests and roll in rather than crash. Notice if the waves form shoulders to ride on. Note where other bodysurfers are catching waves and why they selected that spot over others. You can learn a lot by watching the wave-wise locals. If the beach has a lifeguard, it's perfectly all right to ask where the hazards are and if there's any danger from ripcurrents. As a former beach lifeguard, I would always take time to answer questions and warn bathers of hazards. The rescue I didn't have to make would allow my attention to stay on others who might need help.

Catching the Wave

The principle behind catching a wave with the body is almost the same as for board riding. First, the bodysurfer is using the energy of the wave to slide downward and forward. Next, the buoyancy of the body, like the flotation of the surfboard, allows the ride to begin. With sufficient forward speed, and the right adjustment of balance, the body (like a surfboard) will begin to rise slightly and plane down or across the wave. When you really get moving on a wave, your shoulders and chest rise out of the water and you're surfing.

In bodysurfing big waves or small, the whole trick is to get your head and shoulders *down*. When this happens, the hips and legs rise and your point of balance shifts downward. Gravity, aided by the force of the wave and your stroke and kick, starts the slide. Once the slide begins, and you feel that exuberant rush, the head and shoulders come up. Now the chest becomes a planing surface, and off you go with your body becoming a surfboard.

It's important to be in the right spot to catch a wave. Since no two waves break exactly the same or in the same place, the bodysurfer needs

Michael Kliks backsides a Point Panic, Oahu, wave. Photo: Coco Kliks

to move in and out, right or left to be in the correct position. You have to be aggressive about this and swim or wade forcefully to the best takeoff spot. Skilled bodysurfers are in constant motion as they shift about, jockeying to be where the waves are peaking. If you're too far inshore of the cresting wave it will break before you can catch it. Attempt to catch a wave too soon and the face won't be steep enough to let you start sliding. The best position is to be where the wave is steepest but still unbroken.

On a steep wave where there's a curling shoulder the bodysurfer can sometimes ride across the wave's face. However, the novice should stick to riding straight off in small surf until he or she develops enough skill to bodysurf at an angle. Experienced, go-for-it bodysurfers can slide right or left, turn over in the wave, and ride it on their back. On larger, well-formed waves most bodysurfers and board surfers cut diagonally across the face, trying to race the curl.

The Bodysurf Takeoff

As noted earlier, if the water's shallow enough to stand chest deep, you can achieve takeoff speed and downward body position without fins by pushing off the bottom. Two movements must happen simultaneously.

With arm and hand extended, a Pipeline body surfer drip down a North Shore, Oahu, wave.

First, pushing off the bottom vigorously brings the body level with the water and gives it shoreward momentum. At the same time, take one or more powerful strokes and lower your head and chest, which elevates your hips and legs. This changes the body's center of gravity, allowing the downward slide to start. If you're wearing fins, a few strong kicks will help greatly in catching the wave. Later, with a lot of experience and a "feel" for the slide, waves can be caught with a single stroke and a single kick of the fin.

A deep-water takeoff is almost impossible without fins. The takeoff technique is the same as catching waves where you can stand. In over-the-head depths, you'll need fins to provide the necessary force to raise your lower body and begin the downward slide over the wave's face. At the same time, strong arm strokes will help launch the rider into the wave. Later, with experience, most deep-water waves can be caught with a few strong kicks and a single stroke.

In shallow water the expert might choose to push off the bottom and make a *no-stroke* or *kick* takeoff.

A no-stroke takeoff demonstrates that the bodysurfer has mastered the sport. Wave judgment is the key to no-stroke takeoffs. To catch a wave without taking a stroke you must be right were it's about to break. First, visualize jumping head-first over a low fence or sand dune. Just before the wave breaks, push off the bottom and launch yourself up and over that imaginary fence or dune. As you go over the top, drop your head and shoulders and the downward slide should begin.

Where waves spill from top to bottom I sometimes ride them underwater like a dolphin surfs. An underwater takeoff and ride adds variety to the sport. Dolphins do ride waves underwater, and with practice, so can you. The trick is to duck underwater as the wave rolls over you and push off the bottom in a shoreward direction. Fins help a lot for this takeoff. Your takeoff body position will be shallow and almost parallel to the bottom. Just before your upper torso rises to break out of the water, drop your head and shoulders just a few inches. This will tend to keep your body underwater and sliding forward. I can do this reasonably well, but my son can dolphin-surf big waves 20 or 30 yards or more underwater.

The Pullout

What if, despite your best intentions, the wave walls up as you start to slide and becomes a crasher? Suddenly, you're hurled downward and heading for the bottom at a radical angle. In a microsecond you'll impact violently with the hard sand. Time for a pullout.

The outrigger position looks easy for champion Mark Cunningham sliding a big one at The Pipeline. Photo M.M. Kliks

The pullout is also called a tuckout. When that feeling of being out of control and going over the falls starts, tuck out instantly by dropping a shoulder to create resistance and help turn yourself sideways and into the wave. At the same time, tuck your head into the shoulder for protection, which will further slow you down and allow the wave to overtake you. You'll then roll over, with a hip toward the bottom, and into a sideways flip. If all goes well you'll be facing out to sea and swimming for the next wave.

It's very important to realize that this split-second self-defensive movement is not a forward roll, like a somersault. Attempting a forward roll with the force of the wave pushing you ahead will usually send the swimmer straight for the bottom and a head plant. Very dangerous. A safe tuckout should happen early enough to escape the full force of a breaking sandbuster.

With a lot of practice, and watching how others bodysurf, the day will come when all the movements needed to start a slide, ride the wave, and pull out all come together.

Let's Go Bodysurfing

We'll follow an experienced bodysurfer from shore to catching a wave and get a sense of what she does both consciously and by intuition developed over hundreds of slides. Ann and her novice bodysurfer boyfriend arrive at the beach with a picnic and swim fins. It's a medium incoming tide, which she knows creates the best wave conditions for this particular beach. Today, three- to five-foot swells are walling up as they feel the drag of the bottom. Unconsciously, Ann notes that the swells are arriving in sets with distinct lulls between waves.

Like most macho guys wanting to impress a partner, Brian starts to charge into the water as a set of waves rolls in. Ann stops him and suggests checking the surf first. She points out a rock outcropping that thrusts out of the water 30 yards from shore. Ann mentions that it often starts a wave breaking that has a ridable shoulder. As they wave-watch, Ann notices something floating in the surfline and points out a ragged timber being swept alongshore. She logs the hazard in her memory and decides it will wash away from where they want to bodysurf.

Tactfully, Ann coaches her neophyte boyfriend on the basics of judging a wave, the takeoff kick and stroke, and downward body position, then leads Brian to the surf. She prefers to put her fins on in waist deep water between inrushing waves. She tells Brian that it's easier to work through the incoming white water barefoot. Pulling on fins in dry sand also gets them full of grit, which creates a sandpaper effect on the feet. As the pair slips on fins, a fast-moving wave rolls in, catching Brain unaware. He takes it on the chest and gets knocked down. Ann, always considerate of his ego, faces the next wave sideways, taking the blow against a hip and ribs. Brian, no dummy, catches on quickly. He's also learned never to take his eyes off the surf.

To get through the whitewater where the waves are breaking, Ann motions for her guy to do what she does. She just has time to caution, "Dive under and through it like a torpedo and kick hard!"

Brian, learning quickly, shoves off the bottom and just skimming the sand, shoots under the breaker. By staying deep he escapes the power of the collapsing wave. Being caught in a big wave's impact zone means tons of water pounding and spinning you in a boiling turbulence.

Australian Don McCredie powers across a Whale Beach wave with the help of his own design Hydro Bodygun. Photo Rowan Keegan, Hydrosports, Australia

In deeper water, beyond the impact zone, Ann and Brian float out of harm's way. Ann's attention is always on the horizon. She's looking for incoming swells and maybe an unexpected big one that might break where they're waiting. As an experienced bodysurfer, she can spot a ridable wave approaching as far as her eyes can see. Ann gives Brian a few words about the takeoff and cautions him to pull out early if he senses he's going over the falls. Since the waves are spilling from the top today, Ann coaches her guy on how to ride straight off with his arms at his sides. Later, he'll learn to drop a shoulder and angle across the wave's face.

A steep swell rises behind them and begins to over-balance. Ann yells, "Go for it!" With a stroke and kick of her fins, she starts sliding down the breaking wave's steep face. Brian, mimicking her movements, strokes and kicks, begins the slide, and catches the wave. Ann doesn't expect this and unknowingly angles toward Brian who's riding straight off. They collide in the white water and end up in each other's arms, unharmed. That's a happy ending that could have resulted in a bruising wipeout. Ann explains that angling bodysurfers have the right-of-way. If you're riding straight in, keep away from those on either side who may be surfing across the wave.

They swim back out and catch a few more. Then comes a long lull between waves. Brian's getting cold and starts stroking for the beach. Ann grabs him and forcefully lays down the bodysurfer's first rule, "Bodysurfers always catch a wave in, no matter how cold we get. Got that, Brian?"

In a few minutes a "shore boat" wave arrives and the young couple bodysurf back to shore. Since this is fictitious, the beach is deserted and piles of dry driftwood lay along the berm. Brian quickly builds a warming fire. From his backpack he pulls out steaks, fresh sourdough rolls, a bottle of red wine and . . .

Advanced Bodysurfing

Today, almost all experienced bodysurfers angle across the wave. It's the thing to do, even if there's no wave shoulder to angle on. Cutting right or left adds dimension to bodysurfing, and bodysurfing diagonally across a well-formed wave with a curling shoulder will double your speed, and fun. Angling is also safer in steep, pounding waves because you're partly turned in the pullout position. If that feeling of dropping and being out of control starts you quickly pull out and tuck before going over the falls.

Angling rides on the wave's shoulder are more often found on swells that break off reefs, points, piers and on either side of sandbars.

Sometimes these obstructions will create sandbars or contour the bottom sand to enhance the shape of a breaking wave. The pier at Huntington Beach, California, often has wonderful bodysurfing waves with good ridable shoulders caused by sand sculpting around the pilings. Years back, when lifeguards allowed bodysurfers to jump off the Huntington Beach pier, I had a perfect day there. Several of us would ride in along side the pilings until the wave ended. Where we pulled out, there was a ladder we could scale to the top of the pier. Up we'd climb and then run for the seaward end. Clutching our fins we jumped back in the water and caught another wave in. After two hours of nonstop bodysurfing and ladder climbing, both my calves cramped. The pain was so intense it was impossible to swim. Being helpless and pounded in the impact zone wasn't fun either. Realizing I was being swept into the pilings, I swallowed my pride and waved for the lifeguard on the pier. He dove in and helped me to shore—the only time I've been rescued. If I had stopped to rest before near exhaustion it wouldn't have happened. We all need to know our limits in the surf.

Catching diagonal rides requires a lot of lateral movement to position yourself where the wave peaks. Most waves, even those breaking straight across, will have some sort of shoulder to ride, if only momentarily. The technique of bodysurfing diagonally across the wave is quite

There's room for both surfers on this North Shore, Oahu, wave.

simple. Drop a shoulder in the direction you want to slide. This creates resistance like the rudder of a sailboat and you begin to turn. Very quickly you'll get a sense of how much shoulder movement is needed for the wave you're catching. The larger and faster the wave, the more shoulder drop. Now comes the outstretched arm part, sometimes called the "outrigger" position, that most bodysurfers use in larger waves.

Bodysurfers thrust out that arm because when done correctly it adds to the planing surface. The faster you plane, the higher you can ride on the wave and the longer you'll stay in the shoulder area. When the slide begins, the arm facing the wave is extended full length. This creates resistance and causes the shoulder that's in the wave to drop slightly. At the same time the opposite arm is drawn back alongside the body, thereby increasing planing surface. Many bodysurfers place their outstretched hand on the rushing water to increase lift and gain speed. Since the hand is so flexible it can also help trim direction like a small bow rudder. Some surfers strap on "handguns" on their forward-pointing hand. These planing devices skim the water like the bottom of a surfboard and greatly increase maneuverability and speed. Body-surfing contests are now divided between those for traditional, no-equipment (but fins) bodysurfers, and meets held for handgun users.

Wherever you travel around the oceans of the world, take along swim fins. A day may come, when you least expect, where you'll find breaking waves that call out to be bodysurfed.

...

Nine

...

Bodyboarding

Everyone can enjoy body-boarding. It's pure fun and a wonderful transition to standup surfing. For some, riding a wave lying on a bodyboard is sufficient challenge. Others, as their skills improve, learn to ride on one or both knees. For many, learning to ride a bodyboard becomes a fast-track to board surfing and understanding wave dynamics.

One of the fascinating aspects of surfing is that people ride waves on all sorts of floating devices. Head for the beach and you're likely to find hard and soft bodyboards, air mats, kayaks, dories, sailing catamarans, surf canoes, inflated pillows, air-filled mattress covers, and inner tubes. Almost anything that floats can be surfed shoreward in the whitewater. In the open ocean, sailboats have caught giant swells and ridden them for miles. While a beach lifeguard, I occasionally skippered a 28-foot, high-speed rescue launch and would sometimes surf the boat in a channel where the Los Angeles River met the sea. When the waves were big and spilling smoothly from top to bottom, my deckhand and

A bodyboarder at Sunset Beach looking for the right line.

I would power into a swell and surf the launch for a quarter-mile ride into the channel. It was against the rules, but being surfers . . .

The modern, commercially manufactured foam "Boogie Board," created by innovative pioneer surfer Tom Morey, has drawn more people into the waves than any other surfing device, and that includes conventional surfboards. Many of us who began bodyboarding some years back still call them Boogie Boards. I use the term "boogie" interchangeably with "bodyboard," to refer to the same small and simple, ride-on-your-chest, all-time fun, wave-surfing machine. Bodyboarders are also called "spongers," and the board itself, a "sponge." A skilled bodyboarder on a soft, three- to five-foot-long, five-pound boogie, helped along by swim fins, can perform almost every surfing maneuver—and a few more beyond the ability of stand-up surfers.

Men and women bodyboarders on boogies are riding powerful Hawaii Pipeline waves and getting tubed by big barreling giants as the crowd on the beach hoots with delight. At the Wedge, in Newport Beach, California, bodyboarders take off on 10- to 12-foot-high, impossibly steep waves—and sometimes even make them. Lightweight, portable soft-foam bodyboards have led millions of people into the surf. For some it's a first step toward riding a conventional surfboard, but many world-class surfers are quite content to remain bodyboarders.

Bodyboards, Past and Present

Before today's flexible foam bodyboard became universally adopted in the late 1970s, there were several variations of these short, prone- or knee-riding surfboards. Bodyboards have always had three major advantages over traditional surfboards: They're easy to learn to ride, they cost much less than surfboards, and they're much more portable.

In the past, bodyboarders rode wooden-finned mini-surfboards, called bellyboards or kneeboards, either prone or on their knees. These were an evolution of the early Hawaiian flat-bottomed, three- to four-foot-long wooden *paipos* surfed by commoners. The rigid, flat-bottomed wooden planks worked fine if the rider was skilled and didn't pearl in shallow water. If they did nose in, and the board hit the sand, the back end of the paipo would slam into the rider's abdomen with the force of a boxer's punch. Though paipos were heavy, they could be ridden straight off or angled. A variation of the paipo, the short, maneuverable kneeboard, is still a popular wave-riding machine that skilled surf seekers enjoy. Kneeboards are between four and five feet long and shaped like mini-surfboards. People with knee or leg disabilities find that kneeboards allow them to paddle out and catch waves.

He's a standup surfer on a bodyboard, if only for a few seconds.

This is big-wave, high-performance, bodyboarding.

Many older surfers and beachgoers started sliding waves in the 1940s and 1950s aboard those old air-filled canvas-and-rubber surf mats rented by the hour at beach concession stands. Mats were fun to ride and in experienced hands they could outperform a boogie. A lot of parents pushed their kids into the whitewater and sent them surfing for shore on those inflated floaters. In the 1970s the company that produced quality surf mats went out of business, but the concept of a high-performance surf mat didn't die. Surfing innovators George Greenough and Paul Gross filled the void by creating a truly awesome wave-riding mat. Designed by Gross, the fantastic flexible inflated "4th Gear Flyer" was the result of Greenough test-piloting more than 50 nylon prototypes until the pair was satisfied. The final model was made without handgrips or fins and had three inflated air chambers. Greenough quickly discovered that the mat performed best and would go faster when kept soft. In big surf he would grab the front corners and warp the shape for speed. When Greenough went into "4th Gear," maximum speed, he would pull in front of board surfers and make waves that were impossible for standup riders. These flexible surf mats where a great success. Sadly, the costly, handmade 4th Gear Flyers are no longer produced. If you ever sight one on a wave in the hands of an expert, you'll witness a truly fantastic surf machine. If a Flyer shows up at a garage sale, buy it fast.

The Boogie

Since soft, flexible foam Boogies have been universally adopted as the all-purpose surfing tool, we'll focus on them and how to get the best out of these lightweight wave-riders. Most of what we've discussed earlier about safety, wave-watching, and learning to surf applies to bodyboarding, as does the basic technique of catching a wave.

Back in 1971, so the legend goes, Tom Morey picked up an electric carving knife and shaped the first Boogie Board out of a defective foam surfboard blank. He glued a slick surface of flexible plastic to the bottom and a rough, non-slip coating to the deck. He sold two of them in 1971. By the year 2000, more than 3 million foam bodyboards had been sold by several manufacturers. The trade name and basic Boogie oval nose and concave tail shape has remained essentially the same since Morey picked up that carving knife. In a long-ago *Surfer* magazine article Morey recalled,

> The idea of the Boogie Board was to enjoy . . . to get in there, lie down and feel and really savor the wave. . . . The Boogie Board opened up the doors of life a little more. It caused more people to get out there and wiggle around in the sun and sand, to catch waves and learn about wave motion and to learn about not holding on and clinging to old ways.

Boogies appeal to such a large number of people because not only are they fun and an easier ride than a standup surfboard, they're also safe and portable. Modern bodyboards are fairly soft and light, weighing between five and ten pounds. In a wipeout, you'll only have to worry about hitting the bottom or a surfer riding a hard board.

Bodyboards are made in various lengths, thicknesses, and widths. The foam core of a modern Boogie Board is less rigid than surfboard foam, allowing the Boogie to be a bit more flexible. This also makes them softer and safer, an advantage when body and board connect in a wipeout. Bodyboards have a slight lift in the nose, known as a *kick* to help prevent pearling (see the discussion on surfboard design on page 33 in chapter 2). They also have a gradual nose-to-tail curve or *rocker,* like a rocking chair's support. Like surfboard shapers, bodyboard designers are always seeking improvements to reduce drag, and increase speed and maneuverability. Grooves have been added to the bottom to channel water flow and increase lift. Bumpers have been molded into the nose and tail. To increase strength, some bodyboard builders use *stringers,* additional longitudinal supports, and carbon-fiber cloth. Most boards have attachments to tie on a leash and install fins. Unlike surfboards, with their infinite shapes and styles, good bodyboards hold true to the basic Tom Morey boogie shape. As bodyboards evolved, subtle changes to the rails and rocker have made them faster, more maneuverable, and durable. The bottom skin has become slicker for speed and the top less slippery, though you should still apply surf wax to the deck.

Boogies are sold everywhere. Along both coasts you'll find them in supermarkets, drug stores, chain sporting goods outlets, and, of course, at surf shops. Like all sports gear, you'll find quality and junk. In Boogies, junk seems to prevail at the $19.99 level. Avoid these rigid, non-skinned molded, no-shape bodyboards: They'll set a beginner back months. Go for the real thing, and you'll have a true surfing machine. A low-end quality Boogie that will turn, cut back, and really slide across a wave will cost about $60. Expect to pay close to $300 for a high-performance Boogie, designed for competition, laced with carbon-fiber strands for strength. On one of those wave rockets, with sufficient experience, skill, and courage, you to can take off at Pipeline and snap off consecutive barrel rolls in the tube—crowds and conventional surfboarders permitting.

Selecting a Bodyboard and Accessories

Bodyboard size is important. The Boogie should float you and have enough bottom surface to plane easily. Overly large bodyboards are awkward to handle and harder to paddle. If you're tall and heavy, of course, you'll need an extra large and buoyant board. Quality bodyboards are made in lengths ranging from thirty-eight to forty-six inches. The rule of thumb for selecting the right size is to stand the bodyboard on its tail and place its nose against your body. The nose should touch at your navel, but an inch or so either way won't matter. A bodyboard with a factory-installed leash plug is also a good idea. If you'll be surfing in the tropics, select a bodyboard with a dark deck because they reflect less sunlight into your eyes. Severe ultraviolet eye burns can cause temporary blindness. A bad sunburn can also spoil the next day's surf session.

If you're not wearing a wetsuit, at least pull on a Lycra rash-protection shirt. These thin, skintight jerseys will also protect your chest and belly from the board's skin-irritating deck. You'll need a bodyboard leash and a backup—a short one for average surf and a long one for use in big waves. Bodyboard backpacks are also available. Besides holding the Boogie, you can stow fins, towel, sunscreen, lunch, and a windbreaker, among other things. Boogie backpacks will also protect your wave machine in the belly of a jet.

Surf leash package, designed specifically for a body board. Courtesy Surfco, Hawaii.

Bodyboard Care

The outer shell of a bodyboard is waterproof, but it can crack or delaminate. The major enemy of a bodyboard is water entering a cracked outer covering. As the foam soaks up water, the board gets heavier and performance suffers. Rough treatment may break the water barrier and delaminate the plastic covering. To keep your bodyboard in good shape and free from becoming waterlogged, you should:

- Store the board on its nose to prevent tail creases and delamination.
- Keep the board out of the direct sun. Heat will cause delamination and bubbles may form under the covering.
- Avoid leaving the board in a hot car for the same reason.
- Never use a Boogie as a skim board (a shoreside toy), which will sand the bottom rough and slow the board in the surf.
- Use only hot water and a rag to remove old wax; solvents will destroy the adhesive that bonds the covering to the foam.
- Make temporary repairs quickly to prevent water invasion. That fix-it-all gray duct tape works wonders. If the skin covering begins to delaminate, immediately glue it down with waterproof cement.

Note the leash strap. Nobody wants to lose a board.

Before we kick out to deep water and begin sliding waves, here are a few more thoughts about getting the most out of your wave machine:

- New bodyboards usually have slippery decks, even if the texture is rough. Give the top a gentle scrubbing with soap and water before going out. Then wax the board's deck with a light coat of sticky stuff where your stomach and chest contact the top. Rub on a greater amount where your hands grip the rails.
- Don't let sand get on the wax or the deck will become like sandpaper, unkind to your skin.

Boogie Board Swim Fins

Bodyboarders use the same type fins as bodysurfers (see a discussion on fins on page 153 in chapter 8). Since bodyboarders seem to enjoy the more technical side of the sport, several variations of the classic swim fin have been developed and marketed. You'll have a choice of the traditional Churchills, Viper Duckfoots, the Redley fins favored by

Locked in a fast-breaking wave and about to get tubed or wipeout. Note the boarder's fins.

competitive bodyboarders, and an evolution of the Churchill called a "Slasherfin." Prices range from $35 to $75 a pair.

As I mentioned earlier, the most important consideration in selecting a fin is fit and comfort. Fins should fit snugly with no pressure points. The foot pocket should be soft and flexible. Before purchase, try the fins on in the store, wearing them for a few minutes to make sure they don't cramp your foot. Later, if they seem too loose, pull on a thin pair of neoprene booties to tighten the fit. Look for fins that float. If one is ripped off by a wave you'll be able to find it floating nearby. As you learn to ride larger waves with more punch, you'll want to buy a pair of fin keepers.

Let's Boogie

Once you've learned the basics, it's easy to catch waves with a bodyboard. Riding a Boogie provides a great workout that's truly fun. And, when the lifeguards raise the black ball flag (no surfing), bodyboarders can keep on riding.

Getting Started

The easiest way to catch a wave with a bodyboard is to stand in shallow water and as a broken wave approaches, jump aboard and ride the whitewater. As you jump, push off the bottom to give the boogie some forward momentum. The inrushing whitewater will sweep board and rider right up to dry sand. Most people quickly get the idea of the take-off, slide, and keeping the nose level so the board won't stall, but a few need help.

The weight of a surfer lying atop the board, combined with water resistance as the board passes through, will naturally bring its nose up. Beginners need to be shown how to keep the board almost level with the surface of the water. I've helped hundreds of little kids learn body-boarding, and the number-one problem is teaching them to keep the board's nose down so it won't stall and the slide can begin. Often, I've had to push the nose down as I'm launching them into the whitewater. After a few fatherly assists, kids get the idea and they're off on their own. Of course, excessive pressure on the nose will cause the body-board to pearl. Balance is everything.

Boogies, Little Kids, and Safety

Small, soft Boogies that have some nose kick and bottom rocker are ideal for small children to learn to surf on—provided they stay in the shallows and someone stands watch as lifeguard—and the surf is two feet or less and gentle. Because bodyboards are so buoyant, little kids clinging to them can easily be swept out in ripcurrents, or blown sea-ward by offshore winds, and into deeper, over-the-head water. Be alert to this possibility.

With very young or timid children, I've found it's reassuring to ride on the bodyboard with them. After a few tandem slides to the beach to build confidence, you can push them off into the whitewater for a solo ride. Kids learn quickly if it's fun. A few youngsters are often so stressed and rigid in the ocean that they freeze up and can't get a feeling for the takeoff slide. With practice, and a patient instructor who doesn't project disapproval, even timid kids can learn to bodyboard.

Surfing the Bodyboard

Once the beginner can take off and ride in the shallows, it's time to se-lect the right bodyboard and fins and kick out to deeper water for big-ger, more demanding waves.

You can bet he's thinking, "Do I really want to go out?"

Before starting for the lineup, it's a good idea to practice paddling. Most bodyboarders paddle with an alternating arm stroke, like a crawl swimmer. Since only your chest and stomach are in contact with the deck, the boogie will feel a little tippy at first. The best way to get forward motion is to arm paddle and kick the fins at the same time. You won't go as fast as a surfboard paddler, but with practice you'll be able to punch through, or go around the whitewater and reach the break where the waves are steepest. In bodyboarding, the steeper the wave, the easier it is to catch.

The same before-surfing, wave-watching routine also applies to bodyboarding. A few minutes on the beach searching for hazards, and the best takeoff spot, will be time well spent. If you're like the *Makapu*, Hawaii's bodyboarding fanatics, you'll combine your wave-watching time with a few minutes of limbering up exercises. You'll want to determine if it's close-out shorebreak surf or rolling waves that can be safely ridden. Many experienced bodyboarders like to challenge shore-pounders, but if the waves are breaking on dry sand, don't take off. Also set your course to where when the local bodyboarders are taking off; they know the lineup.

Bodyboarders seem to be less territorial and more willing to share a wave than standup surfers. Perhaps that's because a wave with a wide face will take several boogies without creating hazards for other riders.

In trim and surfing at maximum speed.

Paddling out is a lot easier if you can work around the breaking surf. Plan your paddle out to avoid the whitewater and remember the second rule of surfing: the person riding in on a wave has the right of way, and you may have to eat whitewater to avoid spoiling their wave.

Getting beyond the whitewater to the break can be hard if the surf is pounding. Punching through, turning turtle, and duck diving can all be used. In each case, paddle and kick to gain momentum, then plunge ahead. In a duck dive, get the board underwater by pressing down on the rails with your hands and a knee. Sink the board just before the wave hits, and lower your head. As the wave passes and turbulence eases, angle the board upward. When you surface, quickly get back in the paddling position and move out for the line up.

Get out to where the waves are steepest and about to break. The steeper the wave, the easier it is to start the downward slide. Most times you'll be facing out to sea watching for the swells to rise and become surf. When it's your turn, and there's a wave rising and about to break, spin quickly toward shore. Have a go-for-it attitude. Kick and paddle hard. As the wave steepens and starts to break, press the nose of the board down and keep kicking. You'll feel the resistance of the water trying to raise the nose. If you let it come up, you'll stall. Now you'll need your arms to hang on to the board's sides, its *rails*. If the waves are large and critical, take off and angle away from the breaking shoul-

Typical dropknee stance performed with style at Makapu Beach, Oahu. Dixon photo

der. If you feel that you're losing the wave, push the nose down and keep going straight off to build up speed. When that wonderful sensation of being in the wave begins you can make a bottom turn and race away from the break.

Here's where the fun really starts. On a fast wave, once you've made the turn away from the break, you need to visualize the speed line. On each ride there's a point where you'll be in the best trim for control, speed, and making the wave. By leaning the Boogie away from or into the wave you can angle the board's direction up or down to get the most from the breaker. Use your fins and a hand to help turn the board. If you're outrunning the wave, stall the board a bit by raising its nose, dragging a fin and hand, or both. If you need to accelerate to outrun the breaking shoulder, drop the nose to pick up speed and kick, kick, kick. Like surfing, you'll learn more quickly by watching skilled bodyboarders and imitating their technique and style.

Basic Maneuvers

Once you've learned to catch a wave on your sponge, ride straight off and at an angle, there are many fun tricks to master. Some of the basics

179

In the tube . . . the ultimate thrill of bodyboarding.

we'll cover here are spinners (360s), roll-overs (El Rollos), dropknee riding, and rides in the tube.

The 360. In performing a spin, or 360-degree turn, you complete a full circle on the wave face and ride on. If you want to turn left, look left. Going right, look right. Your eye will lead your body. The turn flows with a smooth continuous action. Start the turn as you head down the wave face to gain speed. Near the bottom and at full speed, begin turning back up the wave face. As the turn begins, release the rail in the wave by sliding forward toward the nose. By now the board should be flat against the wave so it won't catch a rail. Next, raise your legs out of the water and cross them so they won't drag. Now, arch the back and throw head and shoulders in the direction of the turn. If all goes well, and it will with a lot of practice, you will have completed a spinner and can make the wave to its end.

The Rollover. The El Rollo, or roll-over, gets a lot of attention if done well. You can roll either right or left. Starting out, pick the direction that feels most natural to you. However, you'll need a wave of at least three to four feet with some power to complete a roll. This move requires getting to maximum speed before starting the roll. At speed, place a hand next to the wave at the top of the board. Bring the other hand about a third of the way down the outside rail and grab hard. The place to start the roll is a hollow section that's steep and about to break. When you feel the wave going critical, turn for the bottom and slide to the board's inside corner. Then turn hard and climb the wave for it's pitching lip. As the wave pitches out it will roll you away from the wave face and over 360 degrees, and you'll finish right side up and race on. You might want to add some body twist in the direction of the roll to help turn over.

The Dropknee Stance. The dropknee stance has taken over as the expert, big wave–bodyboarder's favorite surfing position. Using this style allows the rider to surf in a semi-kneeling position. You can take this stance on waves large and small. On a wave, the inside knee is placed on the rail of the board closest to the wave. The outside foot is placed forward on the outside rail. This dropknee stance gives good balance and allows the rider to shift his weight for control in big surf. To set up for a dropknee stance, the rider needs to be in trim and heading down the speed line full bore before making the transition from prone to kneeling. When you feel stable, with the inside rail holding well, grip the nose of the board and slide your knee and foot up and on to the board. Then in a smooth, flowing motion bring both knees up on the board and get balanced. Next, thrust the outside finned foot

A bodyboarder heads for some unintended airtime.

forward. Again, get balanced but don't sit on your rear leg. As suggested for board surfers, it's helpful to practice the dropknee stance on the beach before paddling out.

Riding the Tube. Tube-riding is the ultimate bodyboard experience. Inside a tunneling wave all you've learned will have come together and the ride will become pure joy. You don't have to make Hawaii's North Shore scene to ride a tube, though the Pipeline is the ideal place. Getting locked into a barreling blue and green wave can happen anywhere the surf forms tunnels big enough to ride in and out of.

First you have to find waves that curl over and tunnel. A wave that tubes is usually close to overhead and breaking fast. When that special day comes you'll need to position yourself in the lineup quite close to the break. This will take a lot of wave-watching and paddling into different positions to determine the best takeoff spot for a tube ride. The takeoff comes as the wave breaks. A tardy takeoff will send you over the falls. When you've caught the wave and set up your speed run, stall a bit, so the breaking shoulder catches up with you. At the instant the wave throws out, turn up and into the barreling section, and dig in the inside rail. As the wave encircles you, keep adjusting the board's angle

Ever alert, a bodyboarder must make constant adjustments.

of attack for maximum speed. You may be enveloped by the barrel for only a second or two, but that's a major thrill. Before your watery tunnel collapses, you want to blast out the open end and into sunlight to finish your moment of glory. If there's room, drop the nose, kick hard for extra speed, and accelerate out the opening. If you can't make daylight, prepare to get blasted. Sometimes the tube will collapse behind you. As the wave caves in, the air inside will be so violently compressed that it will explode a rider out the open end. Like most surfing skills, you'll get the idea from experience and watching others ride the tube.

The Future of Surfing

Let's go surfing. The wave machine's programmed to spit out Pipeline tubes today."

"Check out my new board. It's bamboo veneer and corn sucrose epoxy–covered styrofoam. All biodegradable!"

"Sorry, Bill, I can't surf tomorrow. My license only allows me in the water on odd-numbered days."

"It's too polluted to surf Malibu, and the health cops are arresting everyone in the water."

"I'm on the waiting list for Sunset. The travel agent says I should get my surf permit in about six months."

These bits of futuristic dialog suggest the possible direction of surfing. Will wave machines, regulated surf access, and rampant pollution, along with surf cops and government regulation, become surfing's destiny? And what about escalating local wave wars? Or does surfing's future lie with cooperation and sharing, the free spirit of aloha, abundant artificial surf reefs and surf parks, and ecologically earth-friendly surfboards?

Surf Parks

Wave machines and surf theme parks are here right now. The Japanese built the first "surfatorium" at Hachioji, near Tokyo, in 1969. Now there are some 245 water parks that pump out some sort of ridable waves, though one knowledgeable surfer we know tells us that only 12 of these theme parks produce waves that are worth riding. That will quickly change as the world's surfing population continues to grow. Increasingly elaborate surf parks will be built to satisfy people's need for adventurous experiences. Surf parks are here to stay, and they offer real wet and tumbling waves rather than down-the-waterslide theme rides and virtual reality simulation.

The next phase of surfing's future will be a rapid expansion of surf theme park wave pools. It's inevitable that there will be high-quality inland surf. The march of big bucks commercial recreation will bring surf breaks with lap-after-lap of continuous computer-adjustable perfect waves to dozens of inland cities. These wave parks will have tropical offshore breezes, palm trees, and arenas under a roof with long serpentine surfing courses. Of course, the artificial surfing experience will cost as much or more than an afternoon at Disneyland, and will be highly power dependent.

Waves of the Future?

Surfers will continue to challenge big waves. Tow-in, kite-in, and self-powered motorboards will allow bigger and bigger waves to be caught. Tow-in surfers are now being launched into open-ocean swells aboard hydrofoil boards that will give them the speed and efficiency to catch waves too fast for conventional boards. There will always be an elite big-wave crew. It's part of surf culture. There's a certain honor and celebrity status that draws people to ride big waves. Is there a limit to the size of a wave that can be surfed and survived? Will someone ever drop down the face of a 100-foot giant? Perhaps, but who can say if anyone will survive a 100-foot wipeout if things go wrong. How big a wave can be surfed depends on the ultimate height of the wave—the only limit to riding big surf is the size of the wave itself. If lives are lost in this quest, as they have been, what then? Should society pass laws, take away the big-wave rider's surfboard, and freedom? We think not.

Friends of the Earth

Earth-friendly surfboards made of non-toxic, worker-safe materials are another part of the future. Most of us forget, or ignore, or don't know, that conventional foam surfboards are a by-product of oil refining. Every time a polyester- and fiberglass-covered board is built, there's a significant discharge of polluting gases into the atmosphere. When one of our disposable, non-biodegradable toys breaks in the surf, the parts wash up on the beach, and if someone picks up the pieces (and please do), they become part of a landfill. How many surfboards suffer the final wipeout each year? Maybe half a million? Like it or not, surfers and the surf industry are causing a small part of Earth's environmental ills.

Thankfully, some board-builders are aware of the health and ecological problems caused by current polyurethane foam/resin-and-fiberglass construction. There's a great future for plant-derived epoxy resins, which are far stronger than conventional polyurethane. Plant-derived epoxy resin allows the lamination of bamboo and other wood veneers to recyclable extruded styrene foam blanks (which melt on contact with polyurethane resin). Because they are made from natural vegetable carbohydrates, rather than toxic petroleum derivatives, this new generation of plastic resins is safer for board builders and less stressful to the environment.

Surfboard designers will also create more versatile shapes that last longer and imitate natural forms. Rick Vogel designs and shapes "Surfsword" boards and fins, inspired by the marvelous body of the broadbilled swordfish. Low-tech, adaptable surfboards for use in all conditions will always find favor among purists. Some really good surfers ride nine-foot longboards for all types of waves. Surfboards are our totems. We need to care for them with the respect they deserve.

Futurists have sounded alerts concerning global warming, rising oceans, and hypertoxic pollution that may mutate our species into extinction. Toxic waste—for surfers and for everyone else who goes into the seas—is a major problem because it causes genetic mutation which effects all future generations of every species.

Global warming, and the rising sea level it brings, seems to be the more realistic threat, or benefit, to surfing. Global warming and holes in the ozone layer dramatically increase the danger of ultraviolet radiation, which means more skin cancers for those who bare their bodies to the sun. With global warming the world's polar ice caps and glaciers are rapidly melting. That's a lot of ice water flowing into the oceans. The oceans have already risen a foot in the last 100 years. In another hundred years, will surfers be sliding waves off the coasts of Nevada or West Virginia? Will land values soar in Denver as the Great Lakes overflow and flood the Midwest? If only the politicians would listen to the scientists. It's true.

What's more likely to happen in surfing's future is a continuation of the twin directions the sport seems to be taking: commercial high-tech development pushing ultra-performances on one hand, and on the other a return to sustainable low-impact, environmentally responsible surfing for simple fun.

Returning full circle back to simplicity and earth-friendly sustainability may be the more satisfying and responsible direction in the long term. Burning through several fragile ultralight shortboards per year doesn't make sense anymore. Companies like Tufflite, Lamboo (bamboo), and Patagonia all strive to create less waste and petro pollution by creating longer-lasting surfboards. Most wetsuit companies are the same by using more durable materials.

High tech can be environmentally positive. The inherent flexibility of naturally derived fibers (like bamboo and wood) laminated on recyclable stringerless foam offer improved surfing performance—and these resilient and superstrong boards last longer. Hawaiian Triple Crown surfing champion Sunny Garcia rides a bamboo veneer board laminated over a non-toxic epoxy extruded polystyrene core. When Sunny rips and wins at Sunset or the Pipeline, people take notice of what he's riding.

Human-Constructed Reefs

Responsible surfing goes back a long way. Originally, in Polynesia, if a tree was cut down for surfboard wood, more trees had to be planted as replacements. Those pioneering surfers were planning far into the future. How many of us plan for more than the next week? Some do. Surfer-engineers are pushing hard to plant artificial reefs on nearshore sandy bottoms, and they will succeed.

Imagine the crowding if tennis court and golf course construction had stopped in the 1960s. That's why we need to create more human-constructed surfing spots. Currently, in Southwestern Australia, near Perth, and on Eastern Australia's Gold Coast, two reefs made for surfing are producing quality waves. In the U.S., Pratte's Reef off El Segundo, south of the Los Angeles International Airport, has yet to create great waves, but it's a work in progress. The perfect lefts peeling off Honolulu's Ala Moana breakwater are a serendipitous bonus from a U.S. Army Corps of Engineers harbor development project. In the future, many more shoreline projects may feature surf-producing contours. Artificial reefs—let's call them human-constructed reefs—do work. The waves they create are surfable, and they'll become a big part of surfing's future.

Many human-built objects such as beached freighters, jetties, and piers create surf in unexpected ways. A few years ago we received a call from a California surfer friend who had been transplanted to New York City. Coming over a cellphone his voice was barely audible over raucous background noise, but we did understand him asking, "What do you hear?"

"Jets taking off."

"Guess where I'm surfing?"

"Haven't a clue. . . ."

"Jamaica Bay, at the end of the JFK runway—that's New York City's JFK, and the surf's five feet and perfect. Can you believe it?"

The Port Authority of New York and New Jersey, which operates the airport, had built a breakwater to protect the seaward end of JFK's runways and unknowingly created a human-constructed surf spot. Our friend, ignoring the mildly polluted water, found an uncrowded place to surf. That's one surfer's discovery. But the JFK break won't handle the tens of thousands of inland surfers who want to ride a wave and share the adventure. Surf parks might.

Which direction should surfing take? Will we have hundreds of wave pool megamalls, surf fashion shows, paid tow-in surfing expeditions, and do-or-die surf gladiators on television? Or a return to the basic freedom and beauty, and timeless simplicity, of our sport? Will we repay the oceans for the free pleasures they have given up? We do have a choice, so let us all choose wisely.

Aloha.

Resources

Organizations

Surfrider Foundation
122 South El Camino Real PMB #67
San Clemente, CA 92672
949 492-8179 Fax 949 492-8142
E-mail info@surfrider.org

A leading nonprofit, activist ocean/shore environmental organization with 25,000 members, 48 national chapters, and 4 International Affiliates in Australia, Brazil, France, and Japan. Surfrider's year 2000 "State of the Beach" is a must for surfers who care about the shoreline, beach access, and protecting surfing areas from development. Check their Web site and become involved.

Heal the Bay
2330 Nebraska Ave.
Santa Monica, CA 90404
310 453-0395
E-mail www.healthebay.org

This grass-roots environmental group was founded in 1985 to fight for a "swimmable, fishable Bay." Heal the Bay has reached outward to make Southern California coastal waters safe and healthy again for people and marine life. After collecting evidence of pollution, they'll go to court to convict the guilty.

Groundswell Society
Glenn Hening or Jericho Poppler Bartlow
5201 Seabreeze Way
Oxnard Shores, CA 93035
805 382-0657
E-mail grndswel@aol.com

This activist grass-roots nonprofit organization was established to create a way for surfers to make direct contributions toward surfing's future outside of the influence of the commercial sector. Hening and Bartlow have created a positive force to counter the excesses of the surf industry and the stress on competitive surfing. *Groundswell Society,* their fascinating annual publication, now exceeds 300 pages of surf-related subjects, in-depth interviews and photographs all without a single advertisement. Join Groundswell Society and make a contribution to surfing's future. The yearly membership of $50 includes the outstanding book and helps sponsor the annual Clean Water Surfing Classic at Rincon, California.

California Coast Keepers/Water Keeper Alliance
78 North Broadway/E Bldg.
White Plains, NY 10604
914 422-4410
Pollution Hotline Number: 877 4-CACOAST

This umbrella of local ocean patrol organizations are committed to keeping coastal waters healthy. These "aquacops" maintain a fleet of boats that daily monitor environmental health along beaches, rivers, and nearshore waters. When violations are found, they take action to identify polluters, gather evidence, and force them to obey the laws. These Coast Keeper groups grew from the Hudson River Water Keeper Alliance, which was largely responsible for cleaning up one of America's most polluted bodies of water.

Surfer's Medical Association (SMA)
P.O. Box 1210
Los Aptos, CA 95001-1210

The SMA accepts members from all the health profession, surfing families, and everyone interested in surfing health and safety. There's even a membership category of "I'll Join Anything Member" for nonsurfers who think it would be cool to join a surfing medical association. The SMA docs are good people to know. Check out their book below.

SMA publication:

Sick Surfers Ask the Surfing Docs & Dr. Geoff
by Doctors Mark Renneker, Kevin Starr, and Geoff Booth

This very useful, information-crammed paperback is truly the surfers' health bible. A must for the traveling surfer and anyone with aches, pains, worries, and questions related to general and surfing health. A lot of doctors who surf put their very best into creating this easy-reading and entertaining book. Most surf shops should carry the book. If not, order from:

Bull Publishing Co.
P.O. Box 208
Palo Alto, CA 94302-0208
Toll-free number: 800 676-2855

Priced at $12.96 plus $3.00 for shipping. Surf clubs are given generous discounts for quantity orders.

Magazines

Wahine
191 Argonne Ave., Suite #3
Long Beach, CA 90803
562 434-9444

Surfer
P.O. Box 1028
Dana Point, CA 92629
www.surfermag.com

Surfing
950 Calle Amanecer
Box 310
San Clemente, CA 92672

Long Board
110 East Palizada #301
San Clemente, CA 92672

The Surfer's Journal
1040 Calle Cordillera #105
San Clemente, CA 92673

Body Boarding
950 Calle Amanecer
Suite C
San Clemente, CA 92672

Tide Charts

Tidelines, Inc.
P.O. Box 431
Encinitas, CA 92023
800 345-8524

Tidelines publishes charts for over 7,000 locations. You can order a full-size, full-color tide calendar for $12.95 plus $2.00 for shipping. Their smaller pocket-size chart should be waterproofed in a baggy and be a part of every surfer's gear bag.

Surf Camps/Clinics

There are several "camps" where novice surfers can become good surfers under the guidance of experienced instructors. Most are located where the waves are good and the water warm—an ideal surf vacation. Like surf shops, they come and go. You'll have to make the evaluation.

Nancy Emerson School of Surfing
P.O. Box 463
Lahaina, Maui, Hawaii 96767
808 873-0264
Web site ncesurf@maui.net

Ms. Emerson pioneered professional surf instruction in California. Besides Hawaii, she has another surf clinic in Australia, which also operates year-round. Her instructors teach all ages on easy-to-learn soft boards that are provided.

Australian School of Surfing
P.O. Box 1228
Coolangata, Queensland 4225
Australia
Phone: 011 61 413 3809 33
E-mail nancy@surfclinics.com

Baja Surf Adventure
P.O. Box 1381
Vista, CA 92085
800 428-7873
Web site www.bajasurfadventures.com

Endless Summer Surf Camp
P.O. Box 414
San Clemente, CA 92674
949 498-7862
E-mail dasurfcamp@aol.com

Costa Azul Surf Camp (Mexico)
Costa Azul Adventures Resort
800 365-7613
Web site www.costaazul.com

Walking on Water Christian Surf Camp
(located in the San Diego, California, area)

6400 Alexandri Circle
Carlsbad, CA 92009
760 736-6679 Fax 760 918-0286
Web site www.walkingonwater.org

Hans Hedemann Surf, Inc.
(short & long board instruction)
2947 KoloKowoove #105
Honolulu, HI 96815
808 924-7778

Club Ed International Surf School & Camps
(Only camp in Northern California. Club Ed also has Baja California
winter tours)
5 Isbel Drive
Santa Cruz, CA 95060
831 459-9283
E-mail edi@cruzio.com

Pure Surfing Experience
(April through October, South Bay, Los Angeles areas)
Camps, surf schools, surf contests
310 546-4451
Web site www.puresurfingexperience.com

Surfer for Missions
(Christian surf expeditions, Maui & Indonesia)
P.O. Box 237
Paia, Hawaii 96779
808 579-8402
E-mail sfmi@shaka.com

Safety Gear
For short and longboard nose guards and soft fins:

SurfCo Hawaii
98-723 Kauhao Pl.
Pearl City, Hawaii 96782
800 755-9283
Web site: www.surfcohawaii.com

Surf Safety Headgear:

Gath Sports Pty Ltd.
(U.S. Distributor)
E-mail headgear@gathsports.com

Odds and Ends

Malcolm Wilson's realistic scale models of the evolution of the surf-board is a just tribute to the shapers and surfers who greatly influenced the sport. His meticulous craftsmanship even includes scaled-down brass screws that replicate those used in the 1930s' Tom Blake paddle boards. The "Waterman" sample presented in this book, and others he created, are available from:

Malcolm Wilson
35105 Camino Capistrano
Capistrano Beach, CA 92624
949 661-1511

Glossary

aggro.   Aggressive surfer or surfing style.

angling.   Surfing across the unbroken face of a wave, either right or left.

ASP.   Acronym for *Association of Surfing Professionals*.

backside.   Surfing with your back to the wave.

backwash.   The seaward rush of water down the beach after a wave's uprush.

bailout.   A planned emergency escape from the surfboard just before an imminent wipeout.

beat down.   *See also* Hold Down.

blown out.   Surf that has been wind-whipped sufficiently to make it unridable.

boil.   A strong upwelling of water usually caused by uneven bottom contours.

bodyboard.   Short foam or wood wave-riding vehicles, usually ridden prone and propelled by paddling and swim fins.

boogie.   A term often used in place of bodyboard. Derived from original Morey Boogie.

bottom turn.   A swinging power turn made at the bottom or well below the crest of a wave.

bowl.   The rising of a wave caused by its sweep over a shallow section of the bottom causing the break to be somewhat harder and faster.

channel.   An area of deep water where the surf doesn't usually break. A good place to paddle out.

closeout.   A wave or series of waves that breaks all at once across the entire face; waves that can't be ridden.

crest.   The top part of a wave. When a wave crests it is just beginning to spill over and break.

curl.   That part of the wave that is spilling over and breaking. Shooting the Curl is riding the wave right where it is breaking and forming a tube or tunnel.

cut back.   To turn back toward the breaking part of the wave.

deck.   The top of the surfboard.

drop in.   To slide far down the wave face to gather speed. To *drop in* on someone means taking off in front of them, usually spoiling the surfer's ride. *See also* Snake

dropknee stance.   Riding a body board with one knee on the deck.

duck dive.   Diving under the wave while holding the board to escape its force.

face.   The unbroken front of a wave.

fetch.   The distance a wave travels from its creation to breaking on shore.

fin.   Winglike projection mounted at the stern of the surfboard to give it directional stability. Also called a skeg.

fins.   Swim fins or flippers used in body and board surfing.

foil.   The distribution of a board's thickness when viewed in cross section.

glassy.   A term used to describe the smooth surface of sea and surf before or after a period of wind.

goofy foot.   A surfer who rides with his right foot forward. (Left foot forward is the normal stance.)

gremmies and gromments.   Young surfers, kids.

gun.   A big wave surfboard, usually over nine feet.

gutter rip.   A swift outflowing of water running seaward down a channel scoured in the sand.

handgun.   A hand-held mini bodyboard that aids a bodysurfer in getting longer rides.

hang ten.   Placing all of one's toes are over the nose of the board.

haoles.   Hawaiian for mainlanders or whites. Pronounced *HOW-lees.*

hold down.   *See* **beat down.**

hot dogging.   Fancy or trick surfing done by skilled riders.

impact zone.   Where the waves are breaking. If the surf is big, the impact zone should be avoided at all costs.

inshore.   The area right off the beach and inside the break.

inside.   The surfing area nearest the shore.

kick out.   Pushing down on the tail of the board to lift and turn the nose over the top of the wave.

kook.   A novice surfer who tends to be disrespectful of others.

leash.   An elastic shock cord that connects the surfer to the board.

lefts.   Waves that allow a ride to the left.

lines.   A series of waves rolling in with some consistency.

lineup.   Where surfers gather outside the break to wait for waves.

lip.   The tip or highest point of a breaking wave.

locals.   Surfers from the same area who surf the same spot.

longboard.   Any board that has the traditional "tongue depressor shape," with enough buoyancy to float the surfer. Longboards are easy paddlers.

lull.   The period of time between sets of waves arriving.

nose guard.   A tough plastic sheath that protects the board's nose and lessens the impact upon collision.

outside.   The area beyond where the surf is breaking. "Outside!" is often yelled to alert other surfers that waves are approaching.

overhead.　A rough measurement of wave size taller than one's head.

over the falls.　Falling down the face of a breaking wave to be driven downward with great force.

paddleboard.　An elongated hollow wooden or light foam board used to travel across the water rather than be surfed.

paipo.　The Hawaiian term for a short, solid surfboard.

peak.　The highest part of a wave, which breaks first.

pearl.　A surfboard "pearls" when the nose drops enough to dig in and stop the board.

polyurethane.　The most common type of lightweight foam used in surfboard construction.

point break.　Where waves bend around a point of land and break with good shape for surfing.

pop-outs.　Mass produced surfboard of usually poor quality.

pop up.　The flowing, standing motion of a surfer coming to his/her feet.

punch through.　Paddling directly into an onrushing wave.

pullout.　*See* **Tuckout.**

PWC.　*See* **WaveRunner.**

rails.　The rounded edges of a surfboard.

reef break.　Where waves break over coral, rock, or sand.

rights.　Waves that allow a ride to the right.

ripcurrent.　A swift flow of water flowing seaward or parallel to shore caused by massive amount of water piling up alongshore that seeks equilibrium.

rocker.　The concave curve along the length of a surfboard.

rogue wave.　A huge wave bigger than any other during a particular day.

sandbuster.　A wave that crashes in shallow water near the shore.

section.　A part of a wave, or to divide. A wave may "section" when a portion of it breaks all at once.

sets.　Waves arriving in a group with lulls between "sets."

sideslip.　Slipping down the face of the wave under control.

skeg.　*See* fin.

shorebreak.　Waves that break on shore usually not well formed for surfing.

shortboard.　A thin, narrow board that is highly maneuverable.

shoulder.　The unbroken part of the wave next to the white water.

snake.　To catch a wave in front of a surfer up and riding closest to the wave's shoulder.

sponger.　Someone who rides a foam bodyboard.

soup.　The whitewater from a breaking wave.

stoked.　Excited, full of enthusiasm.

stringer.　The wood (or other material) strip running down the length of the board. Used for strength and to set the curve of the rocker.

surfari.   A surfing trip, usually beyond one's local area.

swell.   Unbroken trains of waves moving in groups of similar height and energy.

tail.   The stern of a surfboard.

takeoff.   The start of a ride.

tide.   The regular rise and fall of the sea due to the pull of the moon and sun.

tow-in surfing.   Using personal watercraft to assist a surfer in catching a large wave.

traction patch.   An abrasive material glued to the rear deck of a board to increase foot traction.

trim.   To position the board so it planes most efficiently across the face of the wave. A board in trim should be moving at maximum speed and stability.

trough.   The bottom of a wave. The lowest part between the crests of two waves.

tube.   The hollow portion of a breaking wave that occurs when the crest plunges forward to form a tunnel.

tuckout.   An escape maneuver used by bodysurfers to exit a closeout wave.

wall.   An advance front of water without a shoulder to ride on.

walk the board.   Stepping forward or back to change the board's balance.

watermen (or -women).   Experienced and tough all-around ocean sports enthusiasts who can surf, skin, and scuba dive, sail, and save lives when needed.

wave hog.   Someone who won't share a wave.

WaveRunner.   A personal watch craft (PWC) used for tow-in surfing and ocean rescues by Hawaiian beach lifeguards.

wetsuit.   A neoprene surfing or diving suit that keeps the wearer warm. When water enters the suit, the body heats the very thin layer between the neoprene and skin, reducing chill.

whitecaps.   Waves or swells, usually at sea, with the tops blown off by the wind, forming white spume.

whitewater.   The broken, churning part of a spent wave.

wipeout.   Falling or being knocked, blown, or pushed off the surfboard by a collapsing wave or by another surfer.

INDEX